CAE
Practice Tests 1

Patricia Aspinall
Louise Hashemi

CAMBRIDGE
UNIVERSITY PRESS

Published by the Press Syndicate of the University of Cambridge
The Pitt Building, Trumpington Street, Cambridge CB2 1RP
40 West 20th Street, New York, NY 10011-4211, USA
10 Stamford Road, Oakleigh, Victoria 3166, Australia

© Cambridge University Press 1991

First published 1991
Reprinted 1992
Printed in Great Britain
by Scotprint Ltd, Musselburgh, Scotland

ISBN 0 521 42276 0   Student's Book
ISBN 0 521 42274 4   Teacher's Book
ISBN 0 521 42275 2   Cassettes

GO

Contents

Thanks

The authors would like to thank the following people for their help in the preparation of *CAE Practice Tests 1*:

Fiona Wilson for typing the manuscript; Lynda B. Taylor for reading the manuscript and making helpful suggestions; Barbara Thomas, Jeanne McCarten, Peter Ducker, Judith Aguda and Geraldine Mark at Cambridge University Press for much help and support; all the subject officers at UCLES who have patiently dealt with our queries.

The authors and publishers would like to thank the teachers and students at the following institutions for piloting the material for us: Anglo World, Cambridge; The Bell School, Cambridge; Cambridge Centre for Languages, Sawston; New School of English, Cambridge; Studio School of English, Cambridge; Cambridge Centre for Sixth Form Studies; Cambridge Centre for Advanced Studies; Lake School of English, Oxford; Oxford Academy; Anglo World, Oxford; St Clare's, Oxford; Geos English Academy, Brighton; Regent School, Hove; Eurocentre, Lee Green.

Acknowledgements

The authors and publishers are grateful to the following individuals and institutions who have given permission to reproduce copyright material. It has not been possible to identify the sources of all the material used and in such cases the publishers would welcome information from copyright owners.

The Listener for extracts (pp.4, 8, 42, 71); Popperfoto for the photograph (p.5); *Hello!* magazine for the extract (p.7); Camera Press for the photograph (p.82); *The Independent* for extracts by the following journalists: William Hartston (p.10), Danny Danziger (p.32), Peter Bond (p.34), John Ryle (p.58), Ian Harding (p.62), Michael John White (p.82), Heather Couper and Nigel Henbest (p.84); Oxford University Press for the extract from *Traveller's Health* 1986 by Richard Dawood (p.18); Royal National Institute for the Deaf (p.19); Collins Publishers for the extract from the introduction to the first edition of *A Field Guide to the Birds of Britain and Europe* by R. Peterson, G. Mountford and P.A.D. Holborn (p.22); *In Dublin* magazine for the extract (p.30); National Aeronautics and Space Administration for the photograph (p.34); *Where-London* magazine for the extract (p.36); *BBC Wildlife* magazine Vol.17 No.11 for the extract by Chris Baines (p.41); *Which? Way to Health* for the extract (p.42); *The Observer* for the extract by Steve Lane (p.45); Freedom of France, European Parliament Recruitment Services, Eurocamp, BBC Corporate Recruitment Services, Charity Appointments, Wessex Archaeology, Devon County Council, The Stable Family Home Trust, Action on Smoking and Health (ASH) for the advertisements (pp.54–7); Frank Lane Picture Agency Ltd for the photograph (p.58); *History Today* for the extract (p.60); National Galleries of Scotland for the illustration (p.61); Geoffrey Howard (p.67) and Mike Williams (p.96) for the extracts © *The Guardian*; *Business Week Mid-Anglia* for the extract and photograph (p.79); A.P. Watt Ltd for the extract by Paul Heiney (p.86); *High Life* magazine for the extracts (pp.91 and 92).

Drawings by Chris Evans. Artwork by Peter Ducker and Wenham Arts.

In the colour section, pages C1–C8, photographs 1A, 2A, 2B, 2C and 2D are by Richard and Sally Greenhill Photographers; photographs 1B, 2E, 2F, 4A and 4B are by Jeremy Pembrey; photographs 1C, 1D, 1E, 1F, 1G and 1H are from Frank Lane Picture Agency Ltd; photographs 3C, 3D, 3E and 3F are by Abbas Hashemi with thanks to AdHoc Graphics, Cambridge; photographs 4C–4N are from J. Allan Cash Photolibrary.

Book design by Peter Ducker MSTD.

To the student

The practice papers in this book are modelled on the papers of the new (1991/92) examination from the University of Cambridge Local Examinations Syndicate – the Certificate in Advanced English.

Using these papers, with the guidance of your English teacher, or on your own, you can:
- Judge the level of the examination, to see whether it is right for you (see 'Who will take CAE?' below).
- Get to know the formats and range of question types that you may meet in the examination.
- Practise the tasks set in different papers, gradually improving your accuracy and speed.
- Check your strengths and weaknesses in order to concentrate on the language skills which need most effort.

If you are studying on your own, and would like to find out about entering for the Cambridge English as a Foreign Language examinations, you can write to: EFL division, UCLES, 1 Hills Road, Cambridge CB1 2EU, England.

Who will take the Cambridge Advanced Examination?

If you are interested in taking CAE you will probably have already taken and passed the Cambridge First Certificate in English or equivalent examination, and achieved a level of English equivalent to a grade C or above in FCE.

It is expected that most students, though not all, will be in late adolescence or in the early years of employment. If you are younger than this, you will still be able to take the exam and use these practice tests, but may find some of the topics are outside your experience.

The CAE aims to be a practical and relevant advanced qualification relating to the world of work rather than academic purposes. It is useful preparation for the Certificate of Proficiency and is probably best taken at the end of the first year of a two-year course leading to the CPE. You may also wish to take it if you do not want to proceed to CPE but require proof of your advanced level of proficiency in the English language.

This set of practice tests

This book contains four complete sets of practice papers. Here is a brief description of the five papers in each practice test:

Paper 1: Reading (1 hour)

Each paper contains four passages taken from a range of published material such as newspapers, magazines and periodicals. These are tested by a variety of question formats including multiple choice and multiple-matching.

Paper 2: Writing   (2 hours)

Section A: You *must* answer this section. You are asked to read one or more pieces of written material which provide information for you to use in your answer. You will then complete one or two written tasks, producing a total of about 250 words.
Section B: You must choose one out of four writing tasks, and write about 250 words.

Paper 3: English in Use   (1 hour 30 minutes)

You must answer all the questions in this paper. Most questions ask you to provide only one or two words or to put phrases or sentences in the correct order. In the first two questions you must fill in the gaps in the text. The other questions will use a range of formats including multiple-matching. The final question will usually ask you to expand notes or phrases into full sentences.

Paper 4: Listening   (45 minutes)

The listening test is recorded on tape and you will have to answer all the questions. Most texts will be heard twice but the second text will be heard once only. Pauses for you to read the questions and check your answers are included on the tape. There is a variety of question formats including box-ticking, multiple choice/matching and gap-filling.

Paper 5: Speaking   (15 minutes)

You take part in a conversation with another candidate and two examiners. During the test you will use photographs and other visual material and you will be invited to describe, discuss and give your opinion. Most of your conversation will be with your partner.

Beyond the classroom

Try to get as much practice as you can in English. Here are some suggestions for using leisure activities to help your studies:

Reading: Try to find a library that stocks English language magazines on subjects that interest you. Practise scanning the headlines and skimming through some of the articles. CAE tests many kinds of reading skills, not just detailed comprehension, and it requires you to read fast.

Writing: Practise keeping notes in English. If you have time, keep a daily diary; if not, what about once a week? Get a penfriend somewhere in the English-speaking world, or persuade a fellow student to exchange letters on a regular basis. Whatever you do, make a habit of writing in English, so that it comes naturally to you.

Listening: If you are not in an English-speaking country, find out about English language broadcasts in your area. Write to the BBC at Bush House, PO Box 76, Strand, London WC2B 4PH, for details of their programmes in your part of the world. There may also be broadcasts from the USA or Australia which you can receive. If you enjoy music, look out for songs in English where the words are supplied with the recording. If you watch videos, try to get English language versions of films.

Speaking: Remember that the majority of non-native speakers of English use it to communicate with other non-native speakers. If you can't get hold of a native speaker, don't worry! Use your classmates or colleagues to practise with. Try to spend several hours a week using your English to communicate – you'll be surprised how your confidence and fluency will improve.

Results

You will get an overall grade for the examination ranging from A (top) to E. A, B, and C are passing grades, while D and E are failing grades. If you pass the examination, on your results slip you will also get information about which papers you have done particularly well in. If you fail the examination, you will be given information about which papers you have done poorly in.

Practice Test 1

PAPER 1   READING   (1 hour)

Answer all questions.

FIRST TEXT: QUESTIONS 1–14

Read this magazine article and answer the questions which follow it.

SHOOTING PAIN

Did US media coverage of the Lockerbie disaster depict the tragedy or add to it? asks BBC reporter TOM BROOK.

— 1 —

On 21 December 1988, I stood with numerous other reporters at Kennedy Airport in New York, watching a mother writhe in agony, out of control, on the floor of the Pan Am terminal. She had just heard, in full sight of the New York press corps, that her 21-year-old daughter's plane Flight 103, had crashed in Scotland killing everyone on board.

I was there to get a story, so I didn't just watch. I ordered the cameraman I was working with to get a shot of the harrowing scene. The woman lay spread-eagled on her back, screaming, 'My baby, my baby'. The moment was successfully captured on videotape.

At least a dozen other camera crews were zooming in on the woman, who was partly smothered by her husband, trying to protect and comfort her. The press photographers started yelling at the television crews to get out of the way, so that they could get a better look. What we were doing began to feel profoundly intrusive, and possibly inhumane. I didn't have time to think further before a police officer ordered us away.

— 2 —

But, within minutes, TV images of the bereaved woman's anguish were being beamed round the world – which is how her relatives first learned of the family's loss.

The next day, a full-page photograph of the woman, lying undignified on the airport floor, appeared on the front page of the New York *Daily News*.

The short news report I compiled for the following morning's edition of *Breakfast Time* didn't include any pictures of the grief-stricken mother. I cannot, however, take full credit for this. That goes to a colleague in New York who, after viewing the videotape, insisted that the material should not be broadcast. A majority of reporters and editors covering the event did go ahead and transmit the footage. Invariably, the justification was that it helped convey, in human terms, the full horror of the Lockerbie disaster.

— 3 —

The editor of the *Daily News*, F. Gilman Spencer, maintains that, in putting the mother's photograph on Page One, he wasn't exploiting her – just doing his job as a professional 'picturing a tragedy'. The TV station WSTM, in Syracuse, New York, was one of hundreds across America to broadcast the pictures in their local news programmes that night. The station's executive news producer at the time, Karen Frankola, says she decided to use the videotape because 'it gave an emotion – gave an element of the story that was missing'.

The bereaved mother's name is Janine Boulanger. A few weeks after the event, with some trepidation, I contacted her. It was still difficult for her to discuss the scene at the airport. Unsurprisingly, she says it was the most painful moment in her life, and she can't understand why those pictures were so important in telling the Lockerbie story.

At the *Daily News*, F. Gilman Spencer claims that his photograph of Mrs Boulanger did not violate her privacy because she was in a public place when she learned the news of her daughter's death.

To me, that no longer makes sense. It's like saying it's all right to show pictures of a woman being raped so long as it happens in public. When I suggested to Karen Frankola of WSTM that she, too, might have exploited Mrs Boulanger, she made an astonishing assertion: 'Perhaps I was exploiting her. But we do that as journalists'.

4

4

Another, wider question also needs to be addressed: did there need to be quite so many journalists at Kennedy Airport that night? When I arrived at the Pan Am terminal, the airline was making arrangements to brief reporters at a news conference. However, at the last minute, the airline changed its plans, and moved the conference to another site. At that point, the airport journalists had little to do but gather material of those who'd waited in vain for Flight 103. Many reporters and crews loitered in the terminal like hungry sharks, going into a feeding frenzy when they encountered a distraught friend or relative.

5

Most journalists say it's necessary to show human distress at times of disaster. A common refrain from many at Kennedy was that, although they felt uncomfortable, they went ahead because they were only 'doing their job'. Their bosses would have been displeased if they'd returned to base empty-handed.

For my part, I knew it was wrong to be watching Mrs Boulanger in agony that night. Out of respect to her, I should have turned away. And I think many other reporters felt the same way, too. But we didn't turn away. Most of us felt compelled to shoot the pictures to please our editors and beat the competition, and in doing so we only added to the tragedy.

6

People in television argue that the medium requires pictures, but does it have to be so all-devouring? Eli Wiesel, the Nobel Peace Prize-winner recently commented on this while reviewing films about concentration camps. 'Why this determination to show "everything" in pictures?' he asked – when 'a word, a glance, silence itself communicates more and better?'

I think that every reporter at Kennedy Airport could have filed perfectly adequate stories without using the pictures of Mrs Boulanger. I think those who included them in their reports knew, consciously or not, that they had behaved wrongly.

Mrs Boulanger says: 'I almost felt they were barbaric. We distinguish between animals and people by their intellect and their sense of compassion and humanity. In that moment those things were completely absent'. She would like reporters to 'think a little in the future about what they are doing. Is it to enlighten the public – or to exploit the innocent?'

Questions 1–8 consist of statements expressing the opinions of various people mentioned in the article. Mark the appropriate box to show which person in the list below expressed these opinions. (Some of the people expressed more than one view.)

1. After all, it was in effect a public event. ☐

2. Without pictures, the story would have been incomplete. ☐

3. I feel guilty about watching the woman's suffering. ☐

4. Pictures aren't necessarily the most effective way to convey tragedy. ☐

5. Those reporters had lost the moral standards of civilised human beings. ☐

6. I wasn't abusing anyone's right to privacy. ☐

7. Taking advantage of human weakness is part of a reporter's job. ☐

8. I'm so glad we didn't show the pictures. ☐

A Tom Brook
B Janine Boulanger
C Eli Wiesel
D Karen Frankola
E F. Gilman Spencer

Questions 9–14 ask you to choose the correct heading for each of the
sections marked on the text. Answer each question by choosing from
the list A–I and marking the appropriate box.

9. Section 1 ☐

10. Section 2 ☐

11. Section 3 ☐

12. Section 4 ☐

13. Section 5 ☐

14. Section 6 ☐

A	**The Moment of Agony**
B	**Pleasing the Boss**
C	**Exploitation or Enlightenment?**
D	**Justifications**
E	**Why Were They There?**
F	**Images around the World**
G	**Race to the Studio**
H	**Taking the Credit**
I	**A Lone Reporter**

SECOND TEXT: QUESTIONS 15–20

Read this magazine article, then choose the best paragraph from A–G to fill each of the numbered gaps in the text. (There is one extra paragraph which does not belong in any of the gaps.)

Film Star to Auction Van Gogh

Elizabeth Taylor has been busy shedding some of the possessions she acquired during her tumultuous marriages to Richard Burton. She recently sold 'La Noche de la Iguana', the villa they bought together in Puerto Vallarta, Mexico, and now she's put her Van Gogh up for sale.

15.

Liz started collecting works of art in the mid-1950s and always wanted to have a Van Gogh in her collection.

16.

They sought the advice of her father, Francis Taylor, a specialist art dealer.

17.

A year later Richard and Liz were married for the first time in Canada, but chose to hang their precious painting in their hideaway in Gstaad, Switzerland.

18.

The *Kalizma* was often moored in London when the Burtons visited Britain, to ensure they would never be separated from their pets during their travels.

19.

Latterly, the 'Asylum' has hung in her Bel Air home, ever since she divorced Warner in 1982.

20.

It is difficult to ascertain how much the painting will go for, because the market for Van Goghs has been extremely volatile during the last decade.
'A View of the Asylum' is one of many paintings Van Gogh produced during his last year of life while he was staying at the very asylum depicted on the canvas.

A In April of 1963, her wish was fulfilled when she saw 'A View of the Asylum' among some of the paintings Alfred Wolf had put up for auction. At the time she told Richard that she wanted this particular painting 'no matter what'.

B The painting, 'A View of the Asylum and the Chapel at Saint Rémy', will be auctioned at Christie's in London on December 3 and is expected to fetch £10 million.

C Last year alone Van Gogh's 'Portrait of Dr Paul Gachet' sold for a staggering £49.1 million, breaking all the records for a single painting.

D Now she's selling it 'for entirely personal reasons'.

E Following her final break-up with Richard, Elizabeth took the painting with her to Washington DC, when she was married to the American politician John Warner.

F Eventually, they had the state room of their yacht *Kalizma* (a mixture of the names of their daughters: Kate Burton, Liza Todd and Maria Burton) remodelled specially to enhance the Van Gogh painting.

G Francis managed to purchase the painting in her name for £92,000 after cautioning Liz and Richard that if either of them turned up at the auction hall on the day of the sale they would be recognised and knowledge of their interest could double the price.

THIRD TEXT: QUESTIONS 21–25

Read this book review and answer questions 21–25 by choosing A, B, C or D.

The Flatter the Better

Benjamin Woolley

| PETERS ATLAS OF THE WORLD |
| Longman £29.95 |

Though they may not realise, or admit to it publicly, many people still believe the Earth to be flat. Or at least, they believe that the Earth can be made flat, even if it isn't. The evidence for this is the steadfast belief that a geographical map is accurate, that it is a true and fair – indeed, the truest and fairest – picture of the world. Cartographers know otherwise. They know that a completely faithful flat picture of a round object is impossible. Something must be lost in translation – or, to use the more correct term, projection.

The *Peters Atlas of the World* claims to have lost less than others. Though aware that there are no absolutes in cartography, its authors claim to offer at least a truer and fairer picture of the world because their atlas pays proper respect to the non-European countries of the world.

The atlas achieves this by employing a projection developed by the German historian Arno Peters in the seventies, and by fixing on a single scale. Both of these innovations are important because they confront two particularly hidebound, Eurocentric distortions that are common to nearly all other world atlases.

The first distortion is produced by the widespread use of the projection published by the Flemish cartographer Gerhard Kremer (better known by the Latinised form of his name, Mercator) in 1568. The Mercator map, like the *Peters Atlas*, is based on the cylinder projection: basically, all latitudes are stretched out until they equal the length of the Equator. However, with Mercator, the result of this stretching is that landmasses become comparatively bigger the further they are from the Equator. The landmasses to benefit most, in terms of cartographical accuracy, are those at the Equator, which are subject to the least distortion. The landmasses to benefit most in terms of cartographical prominence are the poles, which are promoted from a single point to a line long enough to girdle the globe. This also means that all the northern industrialised countries are increased in size, and that most Third World countries are correspondingly diminished.

The *Peters Atlas* overcomes this problem by introducing further, compensatory distortion: as latitudes are stretched sideways towards the poles, so they are squeezed longways. Though most landmasses end up looking squatter and fatter towards the poles, and taller and thinner towards the Equator, the area they cover on the map properly reflects their comparative size. Europe and North America look smaller, South America and South Asia look bigger, and Africa looks absolutely enormous.

In order to preserve this impartiality, a second distortion common to other atlases has been removed. Rather than show different countries on different scales (usually, Britain and Africa each fill a single page), the *Peters Atlas* shows all the detail or 'topographical' maps at the same scale: throughout the book, one square centimetre always equals 6,000 square kilometres. As a result, the UK is reduced to its proper size, appearing as the merest smudge on the face of the Earth, half the size of Madagascar.

A set of 246 'thematic' maps also help to map a truly internationalist projection of the global society, economy and culture. These yield some fascinating facts. Did you know that the USSR, Finland and Australia seem to be the only countries claiming an illiteracy rate of less than one per cent? Or that Scandinavian countries, along with Japan (and not, as it is often supposed, Britain), are nations of exceptionally enthusiastic newspaper readers? Or that the UK is in the same bracket as Mexico and Egypt in terms of student numbers per head of population?

In the foreword, Peters describes Mercator's Atlas as 'the embodiment of Europe's geographical conception of the world in an age of colonialism'. Though largely true, the low opinion of cartography implied by this judgement is too severe. Mercator's map was developed more as a navigational aid than an expression of European braggadocio (unlike the Peters map, it projects a constant course as a straight line). Furthermore, most atlases now use a variety of projections, not all of which are necessarily Eurocentric.

Nevertheless, the Peters projection and the adoption of a unified scale provides a welcome shift in perspective on a world that has been too easily distorted in favour of the industrialised North at the expense of the rest of the world. Given the more global view required to deal with ecological issues and the shifting of world power, it is obvious that we should all dispense with our imperialist projection in favour of this one.

---

21. What claim is made by the publishers of the *Peters Atlas of the World*?

   A They have researched opinions in the Third World.
   B Their atlas shows the world more accurately than previous ones.
   C The general public has more common sense than cartographers.
   D They have translated specialist terms into more easily understood words.

22. What is the main problem with the Mercator projection?

   A It distorts the relative size of countries at different latitudes.
   B It makes equatorial countries look too big.
   C It gives undue importance to the Southern Hemisphere.
   D It gives a false impression of the distance between the poles.

23. Why does the UK appear half the size of Madagascar in the *Peters Atlas*?

   A It shows Britain's loss of status.
   B This is a true reflection of its size.
   C This reflects the population size.
   D It is represented on a different scale.

24. According to this review, what does the *Peters Atlas* teach us about the British?

   A Fewer than one per cent of the population are illiterate.
   B The British read fewer newspapers than the Japanese.
   C Britain has a higher proportion of students than Mexico.
   D Britain has much in common with Scandinavia.

25. How does the reviewer feel about the *Peters Atlas*?

   A It is ideal for navigators.
   B It is similar to most modern atlases.
   C It offers a welcome variety of scales.
   D It is better than previous atlases.

FOURTH TEXT: QUESTIONS 26–37

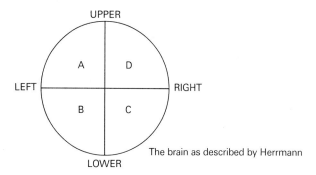

The brain as described by Herrmann

For questions 26–37, read the article from a newspaper which follows and identify which part of the brain will be dominant in the following people by choosing A, B, C or D.

26. someone who buys a newspaper for information

    | A | B | C | D |

27. a famous painter

    | A | B | C | D |

28. an efficient and successful businessman

    | A | B | C | D |

29. an efficient clerk

    | A | B | C | D |

30. someone who is despised by creative types

    | A | B | C | D |

31. a foolish person who always means well

    | A | B | C | D |

32. an unimaginative and unemotional individual

    | A | B | C | D |

33. a brilliant but impractical scientist

    | A | B | C | D |

34. a kind-hearted neighbour

    | A | B | C | D |

35. someone who looks down on good organisers

    | A | B | C | D |

Questions 36 and 37 are about Mr Herrmann. Choose the correct answer A, B, C or D.

36. What is his current occupation?

    A businessman
    B psychologist
    C retired
    D salesman

37. He tries to show people how to

    A enhance the mental powers they have.
    B improve relationships with different types.
    C accept their own psychological weaknesses.
    D overcome different kinds of mental problem.

William Hartston explains a new school of thought on the best way to bring like minds together

Another way to pick someone's brains

DID you buy this newspaper this morning for information, for ideas, because you always buy it, or because you just like it? According to Ned Herrmann, your answer is a reflection of what sort of brain you have, which will affect your working style, your choice of friends and your attitude to change – in fact, more or less everything about you.

Mr Herrmann, 68, is the chairman of the board of the Whole Brain Corporation and founder of Brain Dominance Technology, a theory that has gained him clients among the largest companies in the United States.

By applying recent ideas about what is going on in our brains, he classifies people according to which sector of their brain is dominant. His experience has shown that people of similar brain types communicate well with each other.

While other scientists have concentrated on supposed differences between the left (rational) and right (conceptual) sides, the Herrmann brain combines these with the upper (thinking and analytic) and lower (emotional and instinctive) modes of functioning. The lower, or limbic brain comes from an earlier stage of evolution than our upper, cerebral brain.

If you are looking for vision and creativity, you need someone with an upper-right dominant brain. For calm assessment of ideas and problem solving, upper-left is more reliable, and after that an army of lower-left well-organised characters may be needed to get on with doing the work. Meanwhile some good cheer and support from the lower-right wing will boost general morale. But people of different types really do seem to have difficulties in talking to each other.

The conceptual (top-right) thinker is liable to be disorga-

What kind of brain do you have?

TRY these questions to see how your brain functions:

1. I like to solve problems by:
   a) common-sense
   b) good planning
   c) intuition
   d) imagination

2. My biggest weakness is that I am:
   a) unemotional
   b) pedantic
   c) over-emotional
   d) impractical

3. In a team, my most useful function is:
   a) logical
   b) organisational
   c) interpersonal
   d) conceptual

4. If I find some money, my first reaction would be to:
   a) count it
   b) invest it
   c) buy someone a present
   d) speculate with it

5. Which word best describes your orientation:
   a) facts   c) feeling
   b) form   d) future

The (a) answers are characteristic of the upper-left, unemotional thinking brain; the (b)s represent the lower-left, systematic controlled brain; (c)s typify a lower-right sympathetic, spiritual type; and (d)s are the upper-right experimental spatial thinker.

---

nised and unemotional and would not get on well with a committed organiser (lower-left), whom he will see as a boring plodder. Indeed, according to Mr Herrmann's researches, 'boring' is precisely the word that 95 per cent of top-rights use to describe lower-lefts. Equally, the instinctual-conceptual (lower-right) person may be seen either as an ineffectual do-gooder or a truly good and caring human being, depending on your point of view. And the purely rational-cerebral type (top-left) is either a technical wizard or a total idiot.

Armed with impressive case-studies, he makes out a good case for taking more notice of brains: 240 research scientists working on the American Star-Wars project all turn out to be pure thinkers, balanced between upper-right and upper-left quadrants with not much elsewhere; a large sample of artists all crammed their scores into the upper-right, imagination mode; accountants really are upper-left boring people, and

nurses are lower-right.

By identifying which parts of the brain an individual uses most, Mr Herrmann believes he can encourage them to develop their strengths, while also giving techniques to help develop the parts of their brain that other management theories do not reach.

'The key issue is the management of difference, the acceptance of difference', he says. 'Above all, you must understand and appreciate your own mental uniqueness and the mental individuality of those around you.'

His interest stemmed from curiosity about his own creativity, asking himself how and why he managed to combine his early work as a physicist with semi-professional careers, first as a singer then as a painter and sculptor. Meanwhile he had moved from research in a large corporation via sales to human resource development. Then he discovered the brain, and has spent most of the past decade trying to convince others that it is important.

PAPER 2   WRITING   (2 hours)

Answer section A and section B.

SECTION A

You are on the committee of your local International Club, which, apart from regular meetings, holds a conference in a hotel every five years. This year you have volunteered to help organise the conference. Some weeks ago you sent the hotel a provisional list of requirements, and received the letter below in reply. You have now (6th March) received a memo from a fellow committee member and the note opposite from the guest speaker. It will be necessary to make some substantial changes to the arrangements.

1. Using the information in these three documents, compose a letter to Mrs Granger, explaining what is now required. Write about 200 words.

2. Write a reply to Dr Meads, confirming that you have made the suggested changes. Use about 50 words.

Hotel Dominion

Race Road, Weston, Notts NM6 7BW

15th January

Conference Organizer
Winterslow International Club
Grange Road
Winterslow
BK2 0PL

Dear Conference Organizer,

                    International Club Conference

Thank you for your letter dated 10th January.

We shall be very happy to accommodate your conference this year. Please check the listing below to ensure that we have understood all your requirements. Should any alterations need to be made to these, please advise us in writing as soon as possible. We regret that no changes to reservations of accommodation can be made in the two weeks prior to the dates agreed.

Reservation confirmed

Invoice to: International Club Hon. Treasurer, address as above.
Dates: 31st August - 2nd September

Accommodation: Friday, 31st August: 25 single rooms; 27 shared twin rooms; 1 suite (Dr Meads).

Saturday, 1st September: 20 single rooms; 33 shared twin rooms.

All with private facilities.

Conference room A (max. seating 100)
Saturday, 1st September, 10.00 am - 12 noon.

Seminar rooms F,G,H,J,K (max. seating 20 ea.)
Saturday, 1st September, 2 pm - 4.30 pm.

Catering: <u>31st August</u>
Supper: Informal buffet 9.30 pm
Blue Dining Room (residents only)

<u>1st September</u>
Breakfast: Self service 8.00 - 9.30 am
Blue Dining Room (all conference delegates)
Dr Meads to breakfast in own suite

Coffee: Self service 11.00 am
Conference Room A (all
conference delegates)

Lunch: Waitress service 12.45 pm
Red Dining Room (all conference delegates)
Note: approx. 10 vegetarians (number to be confirmed)

Tea: Self service 4.45 pm
Blue Dining Room (all conference delegates)

Dinner: Waitress service
Hotel Grill Room
Delegates to book tables if required (by 12 noon)
Grill Room open 7.30 - midnight

<u>2nd September</u>
Breakfast: Self service 8.00-9.30 pm
Blue Dining Room (approx. 55 delegates)
Dr Meads to breakfast in own suite

Entertainment Saturday, 1st September: Theatre Trip

A provisional booking of 50 seats for the theatre has been made.
Delegates should be asked to confirm and pay by 15th August.

We look forward to your early reply.

Yours sincerely,

J. Granger (Mrs)
Conference Services Manager.

International Club

MEMO

Date: 6th March

To: Conference Organizer

From: F. Johansson

Final numbers for September I.C. Conference at the Dominion.

Friday, 31st August	26 single rooms
	25 share twin rooms
Saturday, 1st September	10 day-only people
	21 single rooms
	32 share twin rooms

i.e. 63 participants total, including committee and Dr Meads (8 vegetarians)

Theatre trip - 19 would like to go.

All invitations now answered.

NB. Attached note just received from R. Meads —

What a nuisance! I'll contact the participants if you'll write to the Dominion and cancel the Friday night reservations and make the other necessary changes. Pity about the theatre, but we'll have to do what Meads wants, I'm afraid.

Melton College
1st March

Dear Conference Organiser,

Many thanks for the conference schedule. It would have been fine, but unfortunately I can't get away till Sat. a.m. – it's an official visit and I simply <u>can't</u> get out of it. I'm really sorry, as this will mean extra work for you, rearranging things with the hotel, delegates, etc. At least it will save the club the cost of all the rooms on the Friday night.

I suggest that if you give them lunch early, say 12-1, I'll be there by the time they finish and we can get the plenary under way by 1.30. If we break for tea about 3.30, do the small groups from 4 to 6, there'll be plenty of time for a closing plenary, ending at 7 ish. I don't think I explained the need for this properly before.

With apologies for messing you about and many thanks for all your help.

Best wishes,
Robert Meads

P.S. I gather the theatre trip isn't particularly popular, so let's forget that and have a formal dinner on Saturday.

SECTION B

*Choose **one** of the following writing tasks. Your answer should follow exactly the instructions given. You are advised to write approximately 250 words.*

1. An American Senator is going to visit your company (or college) and has asked for someone who knows English to act as a guide for the day. People wishing to be selected for this task are asked to write about the company (or college) to demonstrate their ability to explain in English its routines, facilities, etc. and to give background information where appropriate.

2. Reply to this advertisement which recently appeared in your local paper.

POWERPLUS INTERNATIONAL

Manufacturers of high quality power tools,
domestic electrical appliances
and audio equipment

require

DEMONSTRATORS

for their stand at the forthcoming
International Trade Exhibition

1st – 30th July

Top rates of pay, plus bonuses

Apart from a good standard of written and spoken
English, no formal qualifications are necessary as full
(paid) training will be given.

To apply, write describing yourself and telling us why you
are right for this exciting opportunity.

Send your application to Isabelle Gunter at
ITE (Recruitment), 6 Great Hall Street, Birmingham, UK.

3. For your holiday this year you are going to exchange your home with a family from Australia for one month. In order to make them feel welcome and to plan their visit, you send them an informal letter, in English, describing the locality, giving details about shopping, leisure and transport facilities and any other information that might be useful.

4. Respond to the following announcement which recently appeared in a national newspaper, by writing an appropriate book review.

INTERNATIONAL PUBLISHER seeks books for translation into English. Please send reviews, in English, of fiction or non-fiction works (any original language) felt to deserve publication on the international market, to: Dept. 33, Herald International, Barton Place, London SW3 4FD or telephone 071 223 7701 for further details. Fees payable.

PAPER 3   ENGLISH IN USE   (1 hour 30 minutes)

Answer all questions.

SECTION A

1   *Read the extract below and circle the letter next to the word which best fits each space. The first answer has been given as an example.*

From the moment they leave the security of their *accustomed* environment, travellers are at risk. (1)............................ arise not just from strange diseases they meet on their travels but from other factors too: seemingly uninspiring home (2)............................ such as safe water (3)............................, sanitation and public hygiene controls, legal safety standards for motor vehicles and road (4)............................, are easily taken for granted, but simply do not exist in many countries. Environmental factors such as arduous conditions, (5)............................ climate, and high altitude may constitute a danger; and so may travellers' own behaviour, free from the (6)............................ of the daily routine, and determined to have a good time with scant (7)............................ for the consequences.

When illness or injury occur abroad, travellers are again at a disadvantage – from (8)............................ to communicate with a doctor on account of language or cultural difficulties, or being unable to find a doctor owing to (9)............................ of the (10)............................ medical system. There may be a complete (11)............................ of skilled medical care, or of medical facilities of a (12)............................ acceptable to travellers from technologically sophisticated countries.

When symptoms of an illness (13)............................ abroad do not appear until after return home a final hazard becomes apparent: the symptoms may be (14)............................, may pass (15)............................, and the correct diagnosis may not be considered until it is too late.

	A	adapted	B	accustomed	C	local	D	ordinary
1.	A	Questions	B	Changes	C	Hazards	D	Complications
2.	A	comforts	B	helps	C	cares	D	aids
3.	A	stores	B	collection	C	levels	D	supplies
4.	A	correction	B	maintenance	C	improvement	D	quality
5.	A	worsening	B	unusual	C	sudden	D	adverse
6.	A	restraints	B	assurances	C	certainties	D	regulations

7.	A	knowledge	B	awareness	C	regard	D	need
8.	A	inability	B	difficulty	C	inflexibility	D	timidity
9.	A	misuse	B	doubt	C	ignorance	D	disbelief
10.	A	local	B	district	C	neighbourhood	D	area
11.	A	breakdown	B	failure	C	disruption	D	absence
12.	A	type	B	design	C	standard	D	degree
13.	A	received	B	formed	C	gained	D	acquired
14.	A	unfamiliar	B	unlikely	C	unpleasant	D	uncovered
15.	A	unrecognised	B	unknown	C	unforeseen	D	unearthed

2 *Complete the following extract from a pamphlet on deafness by writing the missing words in the spaces provided. Use only **one** word in each space. The first answer has been given as an example.*

This pamphlet is not about empty statements and false promises, rather it is concerned with the co-operation needed by deaf people from those who speak to them. Any person who is willing to give their co-operation by practising the following points will ....*not*........ only make conversation easier (1)............................ deaf people, but also for (2).............................

Please avoid shouting at deaf people (3)............................ possible. Shouting contorts the face of the speaker (4)............................ the embarrassment of the listener, and (5)............................ the conversation unnatural and strained. Speech is usually (6)............................ heard when it is given in a clear voice (7)............................ slightly louder (8)............................ normal.

Clarity (9)............................ than volume is often the main requirement when speaking. Many deaf people have some ability to lip-read, (10)............................ going to lip-reading classes. Some partially deaf people (11)............................ practise this skill without realising it. They feel that they can hear a speaker (12)............................ when he is facing them. In actual fact this probably isn't the case, (13)............................ they are likely to understand (14)............................ accurately because what they only partially hear is assisted (15)............................ what they also see in the speaker's expressions and lip-movements.

SECTION B

3 *The following text is divided into short sections, and in each section there is one unnecessary word. It is either grammatically incorrect or it does not fit in with the sense of the text. Read the text carefully, and then write the word in the space provided at the end of the section. Some of the sections are correct. If the section is correct, indicate with a tick (√) against the number. Two of the answers have been done for you.*

Anthrax is a lethal disease of livestock that is occasionally transmitted over to humans.	*over*
As a disease of considerable historic significance, anthrax occurs in virtually every country of the world.	1.
It is only a minor health problem, even in developing countries, due to the use of other vaccines.	2.
Lapses in local control programmes, however, can have serious consequences such as the more recent epidemic in Zimbabwe.	3.
The most frequent victims of this are persons who closely associated with raising livestock	4.
or working in industries processing of animal bones, hair and skins.	5.
Anthrax is caused by a bacterium normally present in various types of the soil.	6.
Animals become infected by feeding about on soils where the bacterium is in its growth phase.	7.
Human anthrax results not from contact with the soil but from touching up the tissues of infected animals.	8.
When an animal dies of anthrax, always the important measure is	9.
either to bury or burn the carcass. Failure to recognise the cause of death	√
frequently leads to animal owners in some countries to saving anything of value.	10.
The meat may be eaten and the bones, skin and hair sold or used even.	11.
They may be made into the handicrafts or exported for	12.
industrial processing, and could then become a hazard to people in faraway.	13.

4 Read the following informal note which you have received from a friend. Using the information given complete the announcement below by writing the missing words in the spaces provided. The first answer has been given as an example. You should use only **one or two words** in each space.

I've been talking to that jeweller friend of mine, Jim Carter, who works for Oriental Art Ltd, and he says he could come and give a talk to the institute all about pearls. He says he could bring in bits about how dangerous they are to collect and so on and also show some of the pearls he has collected. He says his assistant could show us how to put the pearls into brooches and so on. I think we could get hold of a film too, which is about Hong Kong and the pearls it sells. Shall we make it the usual Tuesday evening affair at seven o'clock next week - that's the fifth of Feb? I can get Ann King to sell the tickets or we could sell them as people go in. Ann's number is Hexton 223. Give me a ring if there are any problems!

HEXTON INSTITUTE
Lecture and Film Show

"Pearls of the Orient"

Jim Carter ......*of*.......... Oriental Art Ltd will be (1) .... the history of the pearl industry. As well as describing (2) .... and delights of collecting these precious stones, he (3) .... showing some of the most beautiful and rare specimens from (4) .... His assistant will be (5) .... to demonstrate how pearls are used (6) .... the most exquisite (7) .... jewellery and there will be a short film (8) .... Hong Kong, the pearl capital of the world. (9) .... will take place at 7.00 p.m. (10) .... 5th February in the Institute hall. Tickets (11) .... from Ann King (12) .... 223 or (13) .... door.

SECTION C

5 *Read through the following text and then choose the best phrase or sentence, given below, to fill each of the gaps. Write one letter (A–P) in each of the numbered gaps. Some of the suggested answers do not fit at all.*

In common with every British ornithologist who has ever travelled on the Continent, I have often longed for a good handy book on the birds of Europe. (1)..........................., how could I be sure that the woodpecker I saw near Paris was a Middle Spotted Woodpecker? (2)........................... the name of the strange warbler I heard in the woods of north Italy? And I am sure that continental ornithologists must share that longing, (3)..........................., biologically speaking, even more artificial than that between our islands and the rest of Europe.

What are the criteria for a good book on European birds, (4)........................... of the field naturalist? (5)..........................., and not too bulky to travel with, or for actual work in the field. Secondly, it must be fully illustrated, and must concentrate (6)........................... on helping the naturalist to identify the new species with which he is confronted on his travels. Finally, it should be scientifically (7)............................

This new *Field Guide* seems to me (8)........................... Its publication seems to be an event of considerable importance (9)........................... It will promote international liaison (10)...........................; it will help to convince them that the study of the natural history of single countries is insufficient and that (11)............................

I congratulate author and publisher alike on their enterprise.

A a detailed description of the birds of individual countries is essential
B European ornithology deserves to be studied in its entirety
C if there hadn't been an expert on hand
D it is preferably on the small side
E as complete as possible
F in the first place it must be in one volume
G for the boundaries between their countries are
H as the distinguishing features are
I first and foremost
J without such a guide
K based on the latest facts and the best theoretical interpretations
L to meet these requirements admirably
M between the naturalists of Western Europe
N how could I find out
O which will meet the needs
P to science as well as to natural history

6 *A good friend of yours has asked you to look at a school where she is
thinking of sending her son next year. After your visit you made some notes
and now you are going to write her a letter (see next page). You must use all
the words in the notes but not necessarily in the same order and you may
add words and change the form of the words where necessary. The letter has
been started for you on the next page. Look carefully at the example.*

a) school modern – built about five years ago / several buildings, large grounds, trees

b) met headmistress / showed classrooms and laboratories

c) twelve large classrooms / windows overlooking grounds / light and airy

d) biology and physical science laboratories / well equipped, latest gadgets

e) swimming pool heated / swimming all year

f) interested and friendly staff / good relations children

g) pupils happy and quiet – very surprised! / good discipline

h) no time to see where children live / headmistress said children settle down quickly

i) staff take care children / make happy, secure / recommend school

⟫→

Dear Susan,

I've now managed to find the time to visit the school where you think you might send Timothy next year so I'll try and give you as much information as possible.

a) The school is modern; I should think it was built about five years ago and there are several buildings set in large grounds and surrounded by trees.

b)

c)

d)

e)

f)

g)

h)

i)

Best wishes,

PAPER 4   LISTENING   (45 minutes)

Answer all questions.

SECTION A

You will hear a woman calling the tourist information office in a town called Halifax where she is organising a meeting. She wants to book lunch and dinner at different restaurants and she wants to find out what they can offer. For questions 1–12 tick the boxes or put in the prices while you are listening to the conversation. Some of the boxes have been filled in for you and you will find it necessary to leave some boxes blank. Listen carefully. You will hear the piece twice.

	The Bull's Head	Bruiseyard's	Arts Theatre Restaurant
Accepts large groups	1	5	9
Price per head / lunch	2	6	10
Vegetarian menu	3	X	11
Private room	4	7	X
Large groups can use main restaurant	✓	8	12

SECTION B

You will hear a report on the radio warning people to check if they have a certain kind of vacuum cleaner which has proved faulty. As you have recently bought one, you note down the details. Complete the notes by writing one or two words in the spaces numbered 13–21. Listen carefully as you will hear this piece once only.

Make of vacuum cleaner: 13 _____

Model number: 14 _____

May be   15 _____ fault.

Model has a reusable   16 _____

Return to	**17**	branch of Hixons or phone 081-447 260.
They will collect and	**18**	it.
Don't	**19**	it in.
Don't fit	**20**	
Might cause	**21**	

SECTION C

You are going to hear an interview with a woman called Gemma talking about her family. Complete the sentences 22–29 with a few words, using the information you hear. Now read the sentences and then listen carefully. You will hear the interview twice.

22. According to Gemma, some people think that people are like onions because you go through several layers until you reach

    22. _____ .

23. Gemma had always wanted to write a book about her father because

    23. _____ .

24. She didn't think her mother wanted her for two reasons:

    a) Her mother **24.** _____ when she was born.

    b) Her mother would have preferred to

    24. _____ .

25. The interviewer thinks that Gemma's judgement of her mother is too

    25. _____ .

26. Gemma blames her father as, when she was away from home, he did

    not **26.** _____ .

27. Gemma thinks it is easy to love babies and children because they are

    27. _____ .

28. Gemma believes that contemporary society makes it very difficult for

    fathers and daughters to be **28.** _____ .

29.   She found the death of her father particularly upsetting as it meant that

the responsibility for the future was [29.   ] .

SECTION D

You will hear various people talking. There are five extracts which are not related in any way except that everyone is talking about the environment. You will hear the people twice.

Task 1

For questions 30–34 look at the types of people listed below labelled A–H. As you listen, decide in what order you hear each person speak and complete the boxes 30–34 with the appropriate letter. Three people will not be used.

A   a representative from a chemical company

B   people in a supermarket

C   a member of an environmentalist group

D   a farmer

E   a secretary complaining to the manager

F   a householder talking to a council official

G   a factory worker

H   a teacher talking to a class

30.	
31.	
32.	
33.	
34.	

Task 2

For questions 35–39 look at the topics below labelled A–H. As you listen, put the topics in the order in which you hear them by completing the boxes 35–39 with the appropriate letter. Three topics will not be used.

A   the effects of a good summer

B   conserving energy

C   waste disposal

D   gardening

E   testing products

F   the price of 'environmentally safe' products

G   bigger is better

H   traffic pollution

Topic 1	35.	
Topic 2	36.	
Topic 3	37.	
Topic 4	38.	
Topic 5	39.	

PAPER 5   SPEAKING   (15 minutes)

PHASE A

The examiners will introduce themselves to you and then invite you to talk about yourself.

PHASE B1

Candidate A

The examiner will ask you to describe a picture to your partner, who has a picture which is related to yours in some way. At the end of one minute the examiner will ask your partner to say what the relationship is between the pictures. You will then be able to compare your pictures.

Candidate B

The examiner will ask your partner to describe a picture to you. You must decide how your picture relates to it. After one minute you will be able to compare your pictures.

PHASE B2

Candidate A

The examiner will ask your partner to describe a picture to you. At the end of one minute the examiner will ask you to say which picture your partner has described.

Candidate B

The examiner will ask you to describe a picture to your partner. At the end of one minute your partner will be asked to say which picture you have described.

PHASE C

Candidates A and B

The examiner will ask you and your partner to have a discussion about the environment. You must reach agreement or agree to differ. At the end of four minutes you will be asked to report your decision to the examiners.

Read the following suggestions for helping to take care of the environment. Discuss with your partner whether you think these are useful things to do and why. Then decide in what order of importance you would put them, in order to have most effect on the environment.

- Buy at least one 'environmentally sound' product such as biodegradable washing-up liquid.

- Turn the heating down in your house a few degrees and wear more
  clothes if you get cold.
- Return your glass bottles to a recycling collection point.
- Use lead-free petrol in your car.
- Give up smoking.

PHASE D

The examiners will join your discussion and you will be asked more
questions relating to the previous task.

Practice Test 2

PAPER 1 READING (1 hour)

Answer all questions.

FIRST TEXT: QUESTIONS 1–15

Use the extract from a guide to places and events in Dublin to match each of the activities 1–15 with one place chosen from the list A–J in Box 1. It may not be necessary to use all the places in Box 1.

1. go birdwatching ☐

2. see both wild and domestic animals ☐

3. watch and take part in different sports ☐

4. go shopping in the open air ☐

5. buy modern Irish craftwork ☐

6. use a memorial to a poet ☐

7. hear music being played ☐

8. see unspoilt houses in a traditional style ☐

9. see a variety of cityscapes ☐

10. see an exhibition about a famous singer ☐

11. visit an exhibition by an Irish artist ☐

12. learn about eating sensibly ☐

13. learn about growing plants ☐

14. enjoy the sound of running water ☐

15. see work by young artists ☐

	Box 1
A	Phoenix Park
B	Botanic Gardens
C	Herbert Park
D	St Stephen's Green
E	Merrion Square
F	Grand Canal
G	by the River Liffey
H	Central Library
I	Sandymount Strand
J	Bull Island

WHAT'S ON
visitors' guide

Walking Through Dublin Parks

The **Phoenix Park** covers no less than 1760 acres in all, and within it you find the **Dublin Zoological Gardens**, the **People's Park**, a beautiful hollow enclosing a bandstand, the **Wellington Monument**, as well as two major Dublin buildings. During a walk through the park you might catch sight of the deer which still wander through the trees; at one stage the Phoenix Park was a royal deer park. There are also cows, and horses. After Easter the Sunday market starts again, otherwise you can view the polo, or the joggers.

A plan just inside the gate will tell you the layout of the **Botanic Gardens** in Glasnevin. The gardens are built on undulating ground, and there is a magnificent conservatory. At one of the boundaries lies the River Tolka, which completes the scene with a lily pond. This is where the Department of Agriculture run horticulture courses.

Herbert Park lies in the south of the city, between Ballsbridge and Donnybrook. It is separated by a road, which divides it into a smaller northern park, where bowls is played, and a larger southern park where there is a lake, playing fields, an Edwardian drinking-fountain, and romantic hidden crannies and corners. On the north side you can hire the tennis courts for a fraction of the price of joining a tennis club.

Walking Through Dublin Squares

The most magnificent of all Dublin squares is **St Stephen's Green**. The Green opens from the early morning and stays open until the sun sets; around 10.30 pm in high summer, about 7 pm at the moment. At this time of year it is glorious, with daffodils, tulips and a splash of vivid yellow broom. There are ten statues in the Green including a Henry Moore memorial tribute to the poet W.B. Yeats. Two central fountains give aural definition to the square, and benches make it a valuable meeting place, especially as the weather improves. At the north side there is a quiet waterfall, and an ornamental lake.

One of Dublin's most notable squares thankfully still survives unravaged by new and ugly buildings. It's **Merrion Square**, an elegant Georgian frame for one of Dublin's most beautiful green areas. The landscaped gardens are backdropped on three sides by Georgian terraces, and on the fourth you have the National Art Gallery and Leinster House.

Walking by the Water

The **Grand Canal** winds its way past office blocks, wealthy Georgian homes, teeming roads and corporation estates, so giving a total view of Dublin. At Baggot Street Bridge there is a bench dedicated to the memory of the poet Patrick Kavanagh, who wrote:

'Oh commemorate me where there is water,

Canal water preferably . . .'

Sandymount Strand also comes full of literary allusions. Read James Joyce's *Ulysses*, where Poldy catches a glimpse of Gertie McDowell's knickers.

From the banks of the **River Liffey** you can see the **Four Courts**, the **Ha'penny Bridge**, **O'Connell Bridge** and the **Custom House**. On a spring evening the view from O'Connell Bridge of the sun setting over Dublin is one of the most memorable sights this city has to offer.

On the north side of the city a wooden causeway takes you across to **Bull Island** where you will find a bird sanctuary.

Public Libraries

Public libraries make a grand place for browsing, and none better than the **Central Library** in the Ilac Centre, Henry Street (734333). Not only are there books, records and videos, there are demonstrations and exhibitions. At present you can catch the final days of the Rainbow Artists' exhibition, a collection of work from young creative people and an exhibition on Central America to commemorate Central America Week. This will include a series of informational talks and videos. From 2 April there's an exhibition of the work of a Czech artist, as well as an exhibition to commemorate the visit to Dublin of the great operatic tenor Pavarotti. On Monday 2 April there will be a talk by Kay Cunningham, Chairperson of the Irish Nutrition and Dietetic Institute, who has just completed a comprehensive report on this subject. Brenda Costigan of 'Live At Three' will give a demonstration on Thursday 12 April at 1 pm on the subject 'How to Make Your Own Cooking Healthy'.

Galleries: The Malton Gallery

St Stephen's Green has recently seen the opening of an art gallery/bookshop which is an Aladdin's cave for anybody interested in Dublin. There is a permanent exhibition of prints and etchings as well as an exhibition room where different works will be shown. At present there is an exhibition of the work of Desmond Kinney, from Derry. Desmond Kinney is best known for his Dublin murals. Otherwise the shop stocks postcards from the National Library, the Chester Beatty Library, and Dublin pub cards. You can buy Dublin gift items that include Cross pens, Aiden Breen Silver, Failte Crystal and Pewter models with Dublin motifs. All the books are Irish: 'We aim to stock any book that comes out on Dublin.' (The Malton Gallery, Heritage House, St Stephen's Green, Dublin 2. Tel: 766333, Fax: 766123. Contact: Deirdre O'Regan.)

SECOND TEXT: QUESTIONS 16–23

Read this newspaper article and answer the questions which follow.

I was bigger than the entire class I went down into

Matthew Evans is the Chairman and Managing Director of the publishers Faber & Faber.

We lived in a village in Suffolk where my mother was the headmistress of the local school, while my father stayed at home writing and looking after the children. We all went to my mother's primary school, and then, luckily, we all got scholarships to go to the Friends' School as boarders.

The Friends' School in Saffron Walden, near Cambridge, was a progressive Quaker co-educational boarding school, a large Victorian red-brick building on a hill, with the most wonderful, enormous playing fields stretching out at the back.

It was a school where the Quaker ethic of self-determination was tremendously important, so there wasn't any pressure to push you through, and as I was totally preoccupied with football and cricket, and as I actually found the work rather difficult, it meant that schoolwork just wasn't part of my consciousness, and I was doing very badly. My reports would be covered with black crosses, although there'd be the occasional line of praise from the sports master, which gave me infinitely more pleasure than any dissatisfaction with the crosses.

I don't have any memory of my parents giving me a hard time about my work either. My parents suggested I leave school at 15 and take up bricklaying, which they thought was the sort of thing I'd be rather good at, although in retrospect I wonder if perhaps that was their reaction to

THE WORST OF TIMES

MATTHEW EVANS TALKS TO DANNY DANZIGER

my school reports.

But one summer a letter arrived in the holidays saying that I was to be held back a year. I can picture myself standing on the stairs, reading the letter, and being absolutely transfixed with horror at the prospect. . .

Even at that age, you see the implications. Here one was at a time where the differences between age and status are magnified enormously, six months' difference in age was like 10 years now. One really did think this was the end of everything, that this humiliation was more than one could possibly cope with.

Well, I was tremendously upset and panicky, and at an age when one is extraordinarily vulnerable and sensitive, I had to go back to school in September to be with boys and girls a year younger than me, which was intensely demeaning. Physically I was conspicuous, I was bigger than the entire form I went down into. In fact, all the time I felt humiliated, I mean, it preoccupied all my days, and I thought about it a lot at night.

So appalling did I find it, that when we had to queue up in

forms to file in to supper, I always queued up with the form I'd been kept out of. It was revealing of the teachers, because the nice ones would just leave it, but the pigs would say, 'Evans, you're standing in the wrong line,' and so there was then the utter humiliation of being pulled out.

It caused various things to be triggered in my mind which have never left me. A fear of failure, certainly; a preoccupation with making sure that one isn't kept down in life, and a sort of general feeling of unease that something is always likely to happen which could push you backwards.

But what it also did was to make me realise that work could actually affect my life, and I think I became a slightly more rounded and interesting person in some ways. I saw that the world and the way one approached it wasn't seen through the games field, and one discovered a whole new way of thinking and looking at things through schoolwork.

Not that I was grateful at first, I felt very bitter about it all, feeling terrible pain and anguish for at least two terms, a long time in a boy's life.

But school went very well eventually. I became a different person in that I embraced learning and read a lot, and really worked very hard. I got four O-levels – which the school regarded as an amazing achievement – and then I went on to do A-levels, and actually did quite well again, and went to university. I was prefect, captain of football and cricket, and became a rather appallingly well-rounded schoolboy, and one crossed over from being the problem child to being somebody the headmaster came to for advice about other children.

It's probably less traumatic than things which have happened to other people, but it had a fairly traumatic effect on me. It's only now that I realise it gave me a determination to try not to fail, which I might not have had otherwise.

Match questions 16–19 with one answer taken from A–G in Box 2.

16. How did Matthew Evans regard academic work during his early years at Saffron Walden? ☐

17. How did he feel when he heard he'd been kept down a year? ☐

18. What effect did this experience have on his attitude? ☐

19. What result did the experience have with regard to his academic work? ☐

2

A He learnt to like it.

B He didn't really think about it.

C He was very ashamed about it.

D He overcame his reluctance.

E He realised there was more to life than sport.

F He disliked it.

G He couldn't get used to it.

Complete the sentences for questions 20–23 with a phrase taken from A–G in Box 3.

20. During his early years at Saffron Walden, Matthew Evans welcomed his sports reports as ... ☐

21. His parents seemed to react to his poor academic reports by ... ☐

22. Some teachers let him join the wrong queue because they were ... ☐

23. Ever since that time Matthew Evans has been ... ☐

3

A critical of authorities

B afraid of failing

C compensating for the bad ones

D accepting them calmly

E sympathetic

F criticising

G punishing him unfairly

THIRD TEXT: QUESTIONS 24–31

Read this newspaper article and answer the questions which follow.

Quest to uncover the secrets of Earth's ugly sister

A voyage to Venus involves acid clouds, searing heat and intense pressure. The reward, writes **Peter Bond**, may be the survival of our own planet

THE MAGELLAN spacecraft will arrive at Venus on Friday after a 15-month cruise from earth. For the next 243 Earth days – a single day for the slowly rotating Venus – Magellan will drop close to the surface, then soar away to transmit a stream of data back to Earth.

Despite visits from more than 20 spacecraft, including a dozen landings over the past 30 years, Venus has successfully withheld her innermost secrets from curious Earthlings. A formidable battery of defences is arrayed against the best that modern technology can produce.

First is the thick blanket of pale yellow cloud which envelops the entire planet. Before the advent of the Space Age, astronomers believed they were seeing clouds of water droplets comparable to those on Earth. However, spacecraft analysis soon made it clear that they were composed of a mixture of sulphur particles and concentrated sulphuric acid.

Then beneath the layers of cloud is an atmosphere almost entirely of carbon dioxide. Surface pressure is 90 times that on Earth, equivalent to the pressure felt at a depth of 1 km in the ocean. This extremely dense atmosphere retains much of the heat from the Sun, creating a scorching environment with day and night temperatures of around 480C, hot enough for lead to run like liquid water.

Small wonder that the Soviet craft which landed on the barren, rocky plains were able to send back data for only a few hours before they succumbed to the hostile conditions.

Scientists hope that the highly sensitive radar on board Magellan will enable us to see Venus for the first time in as much detail as has been achieved for the other rocky planets.

Why is this mission so important? Venus and Earth were born in the same part of the solar system, and have almost the same size, density and internal composition.

Many scientists believe that we can learn a lot about Earth from studying what went wrong with its planetary neighbour. Scientists generally agree that our world is threatened by catastrophic global warming due to the increase in gases such as carbon dioxide and methane. Venus is a natural laboratory in which to examine theories related to the so-called greenhouse effect.

Analysts disagree about the original composition of Earth and Venus. Some suggest that Venus started off much drier than our planet because it formed in a region of the solar nebula which was closer to the sun. Water vapour was unable to condense and be incorporated into the planet. Others believe that there was sufficient mixing within the cloud to distribute water fairly

evenly between Venus, Earth and Mars.

Whichever version is the closest to the truth, there is no doubt that both planets underwent intense bombardment from comets and asteroids in their evolution. Craters on the Moon, Mercury and Mars bear witness to this saturation shelling. These incoming visitors brought with them vast amounts of water, which was added to the original planetary inventory. Yet today Venus is bone dry while Earth is covered with vast oceans. How did this come about?

There are two competing theories. The traditional view of scientists is that Venus was born relatively dry and with a massive atmosphere. The planet was already so hot that no oceans were able to form, and a dense water vapour - carbon dioxide atmosphere was created.

A different theory has been put forward by the Ames Research Center. They believe that Venus formed with plenty of water. So Venus and Earth may have enjoyed similar environments for several hundred million years.

Unfortunately for Venus, as its water molecules were broken down by solar radiation and lost into space, the oceans evaporated and disappeared. Without water there was no mechanism to remove the sulphur dioxide and carbon dioxide which were continually being added to the atmosphere by volcanic eruptions. For most of its life, Venus has been the barren inferno we see today.

Earth escaped this runaway greenhouse effect because it was cool enough to retain its oceans and because living organisms evolved which were able to remove the carbon dioxide gas. But modern human activity may be creating the nightmare which nature avoided. Greater concentration of carbon dioxide, methane and other greenhouse gases emitted by burning fossil fuels will inevitably cause a rise in global temperature. This, in turn, will lead to more evaporation from the oceans.

Since water vapour itself is a very efficient greenhouse gas, the temperature will rise still further until the cycle gets out of control.

According to this scenario, Earth will rapidly become another Venus, a world totally alien to all forms of life. An unlikely chain of events?

Perhaps, but if Magellan discovers ancient ocean shorelines on Venus, we shall be presented with the most graphic warning of what may be in store for our planet unless we take action.

Complete sentences 24–27 about the surface of Venus with one of the phrases A–G in Box 4.

24. We can hardly see it because of . . .   ☐

25. It is covered by . . .   ☐

26. It has pressure like that of . . .   ☐

27. We know it has areas of . . .   ☐

4
A thick layers of cloud
B flat rocky plains
C very deep water
D clouds of fine water droplets
E liquid lead
F carbon dioxide gas
G very strong sunlight

Complete sentences 28–31 with one of the phrases A–G in Box 5.

28. Scientists still find Venus difficult to explore . . .   ☐

29. Scientists particularly want to know more about Venus . . .   ☐

30. Scientists disagree about the early history of Venus . . .   ☐

31. Scientists made errors about Venus until spacecraft got there . . .   ☐

		5
	A it actually looks rather like Earth.	
	B it has such a hostile environment.	
	C they cannot be sure how wet it was originally.	
because	**D** it may have had a dense moist atmosphere.	
	E there is no water to remove the carbon dioxide.	
	F it may have experienced something like global warming.	
	G they have been unable to land a craft there till now.	

FOURTH TEXT: QUESTIONS 32–37

Read this magazine article about the famous novelist Charles Dickens and answer questions 32–37 by choosing A, B, C or D.

LONDON is steeped in Dickensian history. Every place he visited, every person he met, would be drawn into his imagination and reappear in a novel. There really are such places as Hanging Sword Alley in Whitefriars Street, EC1 (where Jerry Cruncher lived in *A Tale of Two Cities*) and Bleeding Heart Yard off Greville Street, EC1 (where the Plornish family lived in *Little Dorrit*); they are just the sort of places Dickens would have visited on his frequent night-time walks.

He first came to London as a young boy, and lived at a number of addresses throughout his life, moving as his income and his issue (he had ten children) increased. Of these homes only one remains; at 48 Doughty Street, WC1, now the Dickens House Museum (Tel: 405 2127, Mon–Sat 10.00–17.00, admission £1.50), and as good a place as any to start your tour of Dickens's London.

The Dickens family lived here for only two years – 1837–1839 – but during this brief period, Charles Dickens first achieved great fame as a novelist, finishing *Pickwick Papers*, and working on *Oliver Twist*, *Barnaby Rudge* and *Nicholas Nickleby*. If you want a house full of atmosphere, you may be a little disappointed, for it is more a collection of Dickensiana than a recreation of a home. Don't let this deter you, however, for this is the place to see manuscripts, first editions, letters, original drawings, as well as furniture, pictures and artefacts from different periods of his life. Just one room, the Drawing Room, has been reconstructed to look as it would have done in 1839, but elsewhere in the house you can see the grandfather clock which belonged to Moses Pickwick and gave the name to *Pickwick Papers*, the writing table from Gad's Hill, Rochester, on which he wrote his last words of fiction, and the mahogany sideboard he bought in 1839.

It was in the back room on the first floor that Dickens's sister-in-law Mary Hogarth died when she was only 17. He loved Mary deeply, probably more than his wife, her sister. The tragedy haunted him for years, and is supposed to have inspired the famous death scene of Little Nell in *The Old Curiosity Shop*.

If you walk through Lincoln's Inn Fields, you will come across Portsmouth Street, and a building which, since Dickens's death, has claimed to be the Old Curiosity Shop itself. It is thought to date from 1567, and is the oldest shop in London, but it seems more likely that the real Curiosity Shop was off Leicester Square. Whatever the truth, the shop makes a pleasant change from the many modern buildings which line the street.

If you know Dickens's work well, you may like to make your own way around this area, or you may prefer to rely on the experts and join a guided walk.

'City Walks' organise a tour around a part of London which features strongly both in Dickens's early life and his books. This is Southwark, SE1, an area not normally renowned as a tourist attraction, but one which is historically fascinating. When the Dickens family first arrived in London, John Dickens, Charles's father, was working in Whitehall. He was the model for Mr Micawber in *David Copperfield*, so it is not surprising to learn that within a few months he was thrown into the Marshalsea Prison, off Borough High Street, for debt (Micawber was imprisoned in King's Bench Prison which stood on the corner of the Borough Road). The Marshalsea Prison has long gone, but you can stand by the high walls and recall the time that Dickens would go into prison for supper each evening, after a hard and humiliating day sticking labels on pots at the Blacking Warehouse at Hungerford Stairs (near Charing Cross Station).

Off Borough High Street are several small alleys called Yards. These mark the sites of the old coaching inns where passengers would catch a stage coach to destinations around the country. In one, White Hart Yard, stood the White Hart Inn, a tavern that Dickens knew well and in which he decided to introduce one of his best-loved characters, Sam Weller, of *The Pickwick Papers*. Mr Pickwick's meeting with Sam ensured the popularity of the novel which was then serialised in monthly instalments, and made Dickens a famous name.

32. Why should you start your tour of London at 48 Doughty Street?
   A Because Dickens once lived there.
   B Because Dickens died there.
   C Because it is owned by Dickens's descendants.
   D Because it was Dickens's first London home.

33. What is the house like inside?
   A It is still much the same as when Dickens was alive.
   B It houses a collection of books and objects associated with Dickens.
   C It has been redecorated to look like a typical Dickensian house.
   D It has an atmosphere which encourages visitors to relax and read.

34. Why is Mary Hogarth interesting to students of literature?
   A She shared a house with Dickens and his wife.
   B Dickens's love for her was the reason he started writing.
   C Her death is said to be the origin of a scene in one of Dickens's novels.
   D She is supposed to have appeared to Dickens as a ghost.

35. Why should you visit Portsmouth Street?
   A to see a place where Dickens worked
   B to see the oldest shop in London
   C to see the authentic setting of a Dickens novel
   D to see some interesting modern architecture

36. Why was Mr Micawber sent to prison?
   A for accepting bribes
   B for obtaining money illegally
   C for treating his employees badly
   D for not paying money that he owed

37. What is the connection between White Hart Yard and Charles Dickens?
   A He often caught a coach from there.
   B It inspired him to write *The Pickwick Papers*.
   C He introduced the character Sam Weller in a scene set there.
   D He met the publisher whose magazine made him famous there.

PAPER 2   WRITING   (2 hours)

Answer section A and section B.

SECTION A

You have received the following letter from the daughter of some English friends. You decide to pass on some information about her to your former boss, Fred Todder, who has many contacts in different countries. You also decide to ask Katie for some more information (see the notes you've made on her letter).

1.   Write a letter to Katie, telling her how you plan to help her, and asking her to clarify the points you've noted. Write about 100 words.

2.   Write a letter to Mr Todder, giving him any general information about Katie that you think might enable him to find her a job and asking for his help. Write about 150 words.

Yes, said Katie'd done well

I believe Mum mentioned to you that I have just completed my travel and tourism course at St Austell College and I am looking for work abroad from September.
What sort? families? domestic agencies?
Mum said you may have contacts abroad. I would be grateful for any names and addresses you can give me.
What about hotels? shops? not factories etc. presumably?
I wish to travel abroad to improve my languages before, hopefully, going into the airlines. It is my ambition to become an Air Stewardess, but at the moment I am not old enough.
any previous travel abroad?
I have enclosed a stamped addressed envelope for your reply and a copy of my c.v. for you to look at. *Thanks etc.*

I do not yet have all my results for my Travel and Tourism Course as I do not receive them until August. Those I do have are as follows:

Travel & Tourism	Distinction	ABC Air-fares	94%	– Distinction
Selling	Merit	ABC Air-ticketing	97%	– Distinction
Tourism	Merit			

At the moment I am working in the Tourist Information Office in Tuloe for the summer season as this will give me good experience.

Thank you for your help.

Katie Bewshea

Katie Bewshea

```
              C U R R I C U L U M   V I T A E
```

NAME: BEWSHEA, Katie Marie   **TELEPHONE:**   Tuloe (0503) 44321

ADDRESS: 17 Grove Park, Tuloe,   **FAX:**   Tuloe 4040
                     Nr. Liskeard,
                     Cornwall, PL16 4PT   **DATE OF BIRTH:** 11 August 1973

NATIONALITY: British   **NI NUMBER:**   NZ 48 69 15 C

MARITAL STATUS: Single. No children.

DRIVING LICENCE: None as yet, expect to take test in August.

EDUCATION: 1978-1984   Tuloe Primary School
                     1984-1989   Tuloe Comprehensive School
                     1989-June 1990   St Austell College

COURSE TAKEN: BTEC 1st Diploma in Business and Finance with Travel and
                     Tourism options. Subjects studied:
                     Office Procedures   Computer Studies
                     Working in Organisations   Tourism
                     Travel and Tourism   Consumer Law
                     Finance   Communications and Correspondence
                     Selling

QUALIFICATIONS: July 1989 GCSE:

English Language Level 2 Grade	C	English Literature	D
Home Economics (Childcare)	C	French	D
Integrated Science (principles)	D	Mathematics	D
Integrated Science (applied)	D	Geography	D

June 1990 ABTA:

ABC Air - Fares   94% Distinction
ABC Air - Tickets 97% Distinction

WORK EXPERIENCE:

July 1988   Tuloe Primary School (1 week) - Supervised 5-7 Year olds.

Summer 1989   Seasonal Employment - Customer Service and Cash handling.

Summer 1989 &   Harry Bright Advertising, London (4 weeks)
January 1990   Duties included:
                 General receptionist/secretarial which included receiving all
                 incoming telephone calls from clients, suppliers, etc., all
                 visitors to the company, typing correspondence, invoices, purchase
                 orders, etc. and general administration work. I learnt to use an
                 Olivetti personal computer and had basic training on a CRTronic
                 320 (typesetting machine).

September 1989   Peninsular Marketing, Liskeard (part-time).
                 Duties Included:
                 Answering the telephone (customers and suppliers), typing, filing,
                 stock-taking, using fax machine and general administration.

HOBBIES AND INTERESTS:

Catering, reading, handicrafts, and I enjoy a lot of sports. I was a member of both
hockey and netball teams at school. I love all animals and especially enjoy horse-
riding. I particularly like meeting people and spending time with young children.

CAREER AMBITIONS:

When I leave college I would like to work in the travel industry either in this country or abroad. My ultimate aim is to become an air stewardess.

AVAILABLE FOR EMPLOYMENT: July 1991

REFERENCES: Mr. W. Jones B.A. Cert. Ed.   Mrs. E. Bright
                        Head of Business Studies   Harry Bright Advertising
                        St Austell College   10d St Mark's Hill
                        Priory Road   Surbiton
                        St Austell   Surrey KT6 4BW
                        Cornwall   Tel: 081-381 4581

SECTION B

*Choose **one** of the following tasks. Your answer should follow exactly the instructions given. You are advised to write approximately 250 words.*

1.

> The Grand Hotel requires a brief guide for English-speaking visitors on 'Facilities for Children'. The guide should give information on places and activities for children within 50 km. Information should include suggestions for family outings, play facilities, cultural and sports centres.

Respond to this advertisement from a hotel in your area by writing the handout which they require.

2. You are invited to contribute to your local guide book for tourists. Write a short account of one or two famous historical characters who lived in your area.

3. You have decided to sell your house. Write a description of it which you can send to people who are interested in buying it. You should include full details of all the rooms, the garden, if any, and mention any special features. You should also give brief information about the locality.

4. Your company has decided to send one employee on a special advanced language course. In order to choose who to send, the management has decided to hold a competition. You must write 250 words explaining what you would expect to gain from the course and how this would benefit your company.

PAPER 3   ENGLISH IN USE   (1 hour 30 minutes)

Answer all questions.

SECTION A

1   *Read the extract below and circle the letter next to the word which best fits each space. The first answer has been given as an example.*

If you're an environmentalist, plastic is a word you tend to say with a sneer or a snarl. It has become a ....*symbol*.... of our wasteful, throw-away society. But there seems little (1).............. it is here to stay, and the truth is, of course, that plastics have brought enormous (2).............., even environmental ones. It's not really the plastics themselves that are the environmental (3)............. – it's the way society chooses to use and (4)............. them.

Almost all the 50 or so different kinds of modern plastic are made from oil, gas or coal – non-renewable natural (5)............. . We (6)............. well over three million tonnes of the stuff in Britain each year and, sooner or later, most of it is thrown away. A high (7)............. of our annual consumption is in the (8)............. of packaging, and this (9)............. about seven per cent by weight, of our domestic (10)............. . Almost all of it could be recycled, but very little of it is, though the plastic recycling (11)............. is growing fast.

The plastics themselves are extremely energy-rich – they have a higher calorific (12)............. than coal and one (13)............. of 'recovery' strongly (14)............. by the plastic manufacturers is the (15)............. of waste plastic into a fuel.

	A		B		C		D	
	Ⓐ	symbol	B	mark	C	sign	D	detail
1.	A	evidence	B	concern	C	doubt	D	likelihood
2.	A	pleasures	B	benefits	C	savings	D	profits
3.	A	poison	B	disaster	C	disadvantage	D	evil
4.	A	dispose	B	store	C	endanger	D	abuse
5.	A	resources	B	processes	C	products	D	fuels
6.	A	remove	B	import	C	consign	D	consume
7.	A	portion	B	amount	C	proportion	D	rate
8.	A	way	B	kind	C	form	D	type
9.	A	takes	B	makes	C	carries	D	constitutes
10.	A	refuse	B	goods	C	requirements	D	rubble

11. A manufacture   B plant   C factory   D industry
12. A degree   B value   C demand   D effect
13. A measure   B mechanism   C method   D medium
14. A desired   B argued   C favoured   D presented
15. A conversion   B melting   C change   D replacement

2   *Complete the following extract from an article about the Sioux Indians of North America by writing the missing words in the spaces provided. Use only **one** word in each space. The first answer has been given as an example.*

The central plains of North America, east of the Rocky Mountains and west of Chicago, provided the homeland for the Plains Indians. The Sioux, at one time divided ....*into*........ three entities, (1)........................... one of 12 nomadic tribes who roamed the plains. They lived in tepees made of as (2)........................... as 25 buffalo hides each, and never stayed in one place (3)........................... long, moving their camps to follow the huge herds that grazed (4)........................... the plains and to find fresh grass for their horses. The buffalo gave (5)........................... meat for food, hides for clothing, beds and saddles, and the bladder (6)........................... store water. Training (7)........................... early for the Indian children; boys were given bows and arrows, blunt ones at (8)..........................., and girls were taught domestic skills. Work and play soon became (9)........................... and the same thing.

   Although a warrior-tribe, the Sioux fought (10)........................... to secure favourable campsites and hunting grounds, (11)........................... the whites claimed land that was considered sacred (12)........................... a spiritual people. It was in 1876 (13)........................... a combined force of Sioux and Cheyenne defeated the US army at the Battle of Little Big-horn. Five companies (14)........................... the command of Lieutenant-Colonel George Armstrong Custer were destroyed, (15)........................... Custer killed by a bullet in the head and another in the chest.

SECTION B

3   *In the following article about the comparative health of the Japanese and the British all the full-stops (.) and question marks (?) have been removed. Insert the full-stops (.) or question marks (?) where appropriate. You do not need to put in the missing capital letters.* Complete the passage on the answer sheet.

Thirty years ago men and women in Japan could expect to live for 64 and 68 years respectively – substantially less than the corresponding life expectations in England and Wales of 68 and 73 as we enter the 1990s the Japanese have achieved great improvements in their health life expectancy there is now 75 and 81 years here in Britain the figures are 72 and 78 how have they managed to overtake us in health terms an answer to this question was attempted in an article in the *British Medical Journal* (23–30 December 1989, p. 1547) by Professor Michael Marmot and Dr George Davey Smith they were able to reject some possibilities the Japanese don't spend a lot more money on health care than the British they are not genetically healthier (Japanese who live in the United States are as prone to heart attacks as the Americans) the most important differences between Japan and Britain, the article concludes, are the diet and social class contrasts

4 *Read the following information from a holiday brochure about a hotel in Spain. Using the information given, complete the letter on the next page by writing the missing words in the spaces provided. The first answer has been given as an example. You should use only* **one or two words** *in each space.*

Hotel Golden Sun

TORREMOLINOS

The Hotel Golden Sun • Situated above main road, about 500 yards Carihuela Beach • Within ten minutes centre of Torremolinos

Amenities: Large freshwater swimming pool • Palm fringed gardens • Poolside bar • Sun terraces • Sun beds • Attractive restaurant • Lounge area and card room • Coffee/snack bars • TV/card room (videos shown) • Early meals, baby-sitting and high chairs for children (on request locally) • Major credit cards accepted

Meals: Breakfast is buffet style • Waiter service for lunch and dinner • A la carte menu available

Entertainment: Dancing most evenings • Occasional cabarets

Bedrooms: Telephone • Central heating • All twin rooms bath and balcony • 3rd/4th bed available

⠀⠀⠀ >>>→

**Hotel
Golden Sun
TORREMOLINOS**

Dear John and Mary,

I do hope that you're going to join us in Spain. The hotel sounds really good and it's only about 500 yards ...from the... beach and ten minutes (1)............... the centre of Torremolinos.

It's got a swimming pool, gardens (2)................ palm trees, a bar by the pool and sun beds (3)....................... .

There are (4)................... places to eat, (5)............... an attractive restaurant and a snack bar. If it rains we can watch a video or play cards (6)...................... have got a special room.

Don't worry about the children as everything is (7)............... from high chairs to baby-sitting. We just have to (8).................. them.

Then we can go and enjoy ourselves as there is a dance (9)................. evening and even a cabaret (10)................. nights.

The bedrooms are everything you could wish for with (11)............ bathroom and balcony. (12)............... central heating too, although we hope we won't need it!

Looking forward to hearing from you soon.

Best wishes,
Tom and Pat

SECTION C

5 *Read through the following text and then choose the best phrase or sentence, given below, to fill each of the gaps. Write one letter (A–P) in each of the numbered gaps. Some of the suggested answers do not fit at all.*

Archaeologists in Iraq have discovered the world's oldest 'statue' – a stone, standing four feet high, covered with plaster (1)............................ of a human being.

This 'stone man', dating from 11,000 years ago, (2)............................ who were emerging from the pre-agricultural Stone Age into the Neolithic world of early farming.

The statue, probably of religious significance, was located inside a prehistoric house – one of the earliest sophisticated buildings (3)............................ Investigations have shown that the house had (4)............................ clay-coated, lime-plastered walls and floor.

So far excavations have unearthed three buildings containing seven standing stones, (5)............................ retain traces of the lime plaster which once covered them.

However, (6)............................ shows evidence of having been shaped into the likeness of a human being. It is 30 centuries older (7)............................ previously known oldest statue. (8)............................ that each building appears to have had at least one standing stone inside it, and that one house actually had three.

The plaster-covered human shaped obelisk (9)............................ shoulders and the stumps of arms and part of a neck. The 'head', however, (10).............................

A   ever discovered by archaeologists
B   moulded into the shape
C   to have been built
D   strangely carved
E   was fashioned by a people
F   excavations have revealed
G   only one of these
H   neither of them
I   beautifully finished
J   than the remaining
K   has what appear to be
L   seems to have broken off
M   four of which
N   has been missing
O   it has been decided
P   than the world's

6   *You have had a very unsatisfactory holiday in Greece with your family and you are going to write to the travel company to complain. While you were away you kept some notes to remind you of the problems and now you are going to write a letter to the travel company. You must use all the words in the notes but not necessarily in the same order and you may add words and change the form of the words where necessary. Look carefully at the example that has been done for you.*

a)   Kephalonia Travel Ltd / two weeks / July / Gatwick Airport

b)   plane delayed / four hours / no information / unhelpful airport staff

c)   flight uncomfortable / cold food / air hostess rude

d)   landed midnight / no bus / taxi expensive / hotel closed

e)   hotel manager grumpy / room not ready / no hot water

f)   breakfast inadequate / only coffee / bread stale

g)   hotel far from beach / beach dirty / only one restaurant

h)   weather very hot / rooms lacked air-conditioning / mosquitoes

i)   dreadful holiday / explanation required / money back

a)

```
                                    27 Edward Street
                                    King's Lynn
                                    Norfolk

    Dear Sir

    I recently took a holiday with Kephalonia Travel Ltd for two
    weeks in July, flying from Gatwick Airport.
```

b)

c)

d)

e)

f)

g)

h)

i)

```
    Yours faithfully,
```

PAPER 4   LISTENING   (45 minutes)

Answer all questions.

SECTION A

You will hear a news item in which an accident involving a young girl is described. Look at the pictures below and decide which ones show what actually happened. Some of the pictures are not correct. The first time you listen, put a cross against any pictures which are not correct. The second time you listen, put the correct pictures in the right order by putting 1 against the first picture you hear, 2 against the second picture, etc. Listen carefully. You will hear the piece twice.

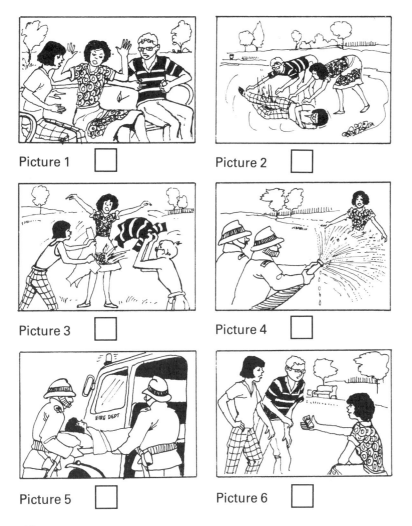

Picture 1 ☐   Picture 2 ☐

Picture 3 ☐   Picture 4 ☐

Picture 5 ☐   Picture 6 ☐

SECTION B

You will hear an information announcement about facilities offered at Schipol Airport in Amsterdam. Look at the sentences numbered 7–16 and complete them by writing one or two words in the spaces. Listen carefully as you will hear this piece once only.

7. The main transfer desks are situated in the

   | 7. | |

8. The most up-to-date departure information is on the

   | 8. | |

9. There are over | 9. | shops in the award-

   winning, | 9. | shopping centre.

10. All the shops have copies of the | 10. | .

11. The airport's conference rooms are | 11. |

    and | 11. | .

12. Additional facilities on the | 12. | include

    | 12. | and a nursery.

13. The railway station is located | 13. |

    opposite the terminal building.

14. You can reach the railway station via the | 14. | .

15. Trains to Amsterdam depart every | 15. | .

    Return fare is | 15. | Dutch guilders.

16. | 16. | 'Centraal Nederland' buses depart

    from in front of the | 16. | .

SECTION C

You will hear an interview between a manager and a member of her staff. Answer questions 17–21 by ticking the best answer A, B, C or D. You will hear the interview twice.

17. Why is Dorothy dissatisfied with Natalie's schedules?
     A   Natalie has not said when the jobs will be done.
     B   Natalie has not estimated how much it will cost.
     C   Natalie has not had enough time to complete her objectives.
     D   Natalie has made some mistakes in her estimates.

18. What does Natalie feel about the schedules?
     A   regretful that she hasn't completed them
     B   content to leave them as they are
     C   unhappy to have irritated her manager
     D   frustrated at being given the task

19. Why does Dorothy say she needs the schedules?
     A   to give to the director
     B   to improve the quality of the products
     C   to help staff to plan their work
     D   to reduce workloads

20. What does Natalie regard as the most important part of her job?
     A   ensuring that the products are top quality
     B   arranging meetings with other departments
     C   talking to the customers
     D   encouraging colleagues to work more efficiently

21. When Natalie says 'Oh, here we go . . .', she is commenting on
     A   the language being used.
     B   the number of products she is responsible for.
     C   being contacted by her manager.
     D   being made to finish the task.

SECTION D

You will hear various people talking. There are five extracts which are not related in any way except that everyone is talking about experiences they have had. You will hear the people twice.

Task 1

For questions 22–26 look at the topics below labelled A–H. As you listen, put the topics in the order in which you hear them by completing the boxes 22–26 with the appropriate letter. Three topics will not be used.

A   solitary confinement

B   people's attitude to the disabled

C   memory

D   a marvellous surprise

E   becoming a writer

F   looking after the elderly

G   an earthquake disaster

H   marriage

Topic 1	22.
Topic 2	23.
Topic 3	24.
Topic 4	25.
Topic 5	26.

Task 2

For questions 27–31 look at the types of people listed below labelled A–H. As you listen, decide in what order you hear each person speak and complete the boxes 27–31 with the appropriate letter. Three people will not be used.

A   a proud parent

B   a long-lost relative

C   a kidnap victim

D   an author

E   a blind woman

F   a man in a wheelchair

G   a psychiatrist

H   a nurse

27.	
28.	
29.	
30.	
31.	

PAPER 5 SPEAKING (15 minutes)

PHASE A

The examiners will introduce themselves to you and then invite you to talk about yourself.

PHASE B1

Candidate A

The examiner will ask you to describe a picture to your partner. At the end of one minute your partner will be asked to say which picture you have described.

Candidate B

The examiner will ask your partner to describe a picture to you. At the end of one minute the examiner will ask you to say which picture your partner has described.

PHASE B2

Candidate A

The examiner will ask your partner to describe a picture to you. You must decide how your picture relates to it. After one minute you will be able to compare your pictures.

Candidate B

The examiner will ask you to describe a picture to your partner, who has a picture which is related to yours in some way. At the end of one minute the examiner will ask your partner to say what the relationship is between the pictures. You will then be able to compare your pictures.

PHASE C

Candidates A and B

The examiner will ask you and your partner to have a discussion about 'Qualities in a travelling companion'. You must reach agreement or agree to differ. At the end of four minutes you will be asked to report your decision to the examiners.

Imagine that you are planning to spend a year travelling round the world. With your partner, discuss the qualities listed below and try to agree on their order of importance.

Qualities in a Travelling Companion

- sense of humour
- knowledge of languages
- even-tempered
- highly organised
- brave
- a good singing voice
- trained in self-defence
- very fit
- experienced traveller
- careful with money

PHASE D

The examiners will join your discussion and you will be asked more questions relating to the previous task.

Practice Test 3

PAPER 1   READING   (1 hour)

Answer all questions.

FIRST TEXT: QUESTIONS 1–14

Look at the advertisements which come from the appointments sections of newspapers, then answer the questions by choosing A–I.

A

JOBS IN FRANCE

Freedom of France is one of Britains Specialist luxury self-drive, self-catering camping holiday operators in France.

Campsite Couriers are needed for the period late April to mid-September. The ability to speak French would be an advantage but it is essential that you are over 20 and available for the full period. Duties include welcoming the guests and ensuring they have an enjoyable stay and that their tents are in a clean and tidy condition prior to their arrival. In addition Freedom of France offers a comprehensive package of children's entertainment and the Campsite Couriers are responsible for organising this. At some sites we offer a watersports option so some Canoeists / Sailors / Windsurfers are also required.

Application form & further details from Mick Fryer

FREEDOM·OF·FRANCE
Alton Court,
Penyard Lane (893),
Ross-on-Wye,
Herefordshire, HR9 5NR.
Tel: (0989) 764211

B

The Secretariat of the EUROPEAN PARLIAMENT in LUXEMBOURG

is organizing an open competition to recruit

Interpreters

English-language (f/m)

Principal conditions of eligibility:
- ☐ university degree or equivalent professional experience;
- ☐ training or experience as a conference interpreter;
- ☐ perfect command of English and thorough knowledge of Spanish or Portuguese and of two other official languages of the European Community. Knowledge of a fifth official language of the European Community is desirable;
- ☐ candidates must be nationals of one of the Member States of the European Community;
- ☐ age: not more than 40 (born after 5 November 1949). Derogations raising the age limit by up to six years may be granted under certain conditions.

The European Parliament is an equal opportunities employer.

Place of employment: Luxembourg or Brussels.

The issue of the Official Journal containing the mandatory application form and all the necessary information may be obtained by writing, on postcards only, **quoting reference PE/148/LA:**
- to the European Parliament Information Office, 2 Queen Anne's Gate, London SW1H 9AA,
- or to the European Parliament, Recruitment Service, L-2929 Luxembourg.

Closing date for applications: 5 November 1990.

C

1000 SUMMER JOBS IN EUROPE

If you'd like the challenge of working at a European resort during summer 1991, Eurocamp would like to talk with you. As one of Europe's leading Tour Operators we have over 1,000 jobs available for:-

COURIER • SENIOR COURIER • SITE SUPERVISOR

You'll need energy, self motivation, an outgoing personality and some knowledge of a major European language. If you're over 18 and looking for a summer job with real rewards, apply today to:- **Richard Layfield, Courier Department, G13, Eurocamp, Edmundson House, Tatton Street, Knutsford, Cheshire WA16 6BG**

Eurocamp

D

Co-ordinator Czechoslovakia

BBC World Service   World Service Training

BBC World Service is currently running a series of schemes for television and radio colleagues from Poland and Hungary to show them how the media operates within the UK. In April a similar scheme for Czechoslovakia will begin and we need someone for one year to run it. You will need to have extensive experience of working in radio or television, a knowledge of the issues currently facing the media in the UK and a real interest in the developments taking place in East and Central Europe.

Offered as a one year contract. Salary will be negotiable and not less than £22,500 p.a. Based Central London.

For further information please phone **Gwyneth Henderson on 071-257 2024**. Please phone or write for an application form to the **World Service Recruitment Office, Room 111 NE, Bush House, Strand, London WC2B 4PH, Tel: 071-257 2948**, (quoting ref: 6853/G enclose s.a.e.).

We welcome applications from men and women irrespective of race, creed or colour.

Application forms to be returned by February 4th.

WE ARE AN EQUAL OPPORTUNITIES EMPLOYER

E

APPEAL DIRECTOR
GAP ACTIVITY PROJECTS

GAP, an educational charity based in Reading, requires a full-time Appeal Director from October 1990. GAP arranges voluntary work placements for young people all over the world.

Candidate must have outstanding communication skills, confidence and initiative. WP skills essential, knowledge of spreadsheet and database an advantage **Salary c.£13K.**

Write with full CV to John Huckstep, Charity Appointments, 3 Spital Yard, London E1 6AQ.

Charity Appointments
A registered charity serving the voluntary sector

F

WESSEX ARCHAEOLOGY PROJECT
DEVELOPMENT OFFICER

This new post will involve promotion, development and tendering for new projects, advising clients on appropriate archaeological action and project management.

Considerable experience is required in field archaeology, estimating, archaeological and planning policies and management.

Candidates must possess a good relevant degree, a full driving licence and membership of I.F.A.

Salary in the range £16,014 - £20,000 p.a., generous pension scheme. Assistance may be given with removal expenses.

Applications in writing with a full C.V. and details of two referees by 10th October to:

DIRECTOR
WESSEX ARCHAEOLOGY
PORTWAY HOUSE
SOUTH PORTWAY ESTATE
OLD SARUM Nr SALISBURY
WILTSHIRE SP4 6EB

G

Area County Secretary
Up to £29,500
+ Lease car
Plymouth

A Solicitor or Barrister is required to head a legal office for the Council based in Plymouth. The office serves a large area of West Devon including Plymouth, with a population of about 400,000. Experience of childcare work is essential; other local government experience is desirable. Excellent opportunity to gain experience in managing a small office.

Application form and further details plus those of car lease scheme, removal expenses and other benefits from the County Solicitor's Department, Devon County Council, County Hall, Topsham Road, Exeter EX2 4QB. Tel: Exeter (0392) 382323 (24 hour answerphone).

Closing date:22nd October 1990

Devon
COUNTY COUNCIL
Devon is an equal opportunities employer.

H

THE STABLE
FAMILY HOME TRUST
RINGWOOD, HAMPSHIRE

DIRECTOR

This well established Charitable Trust, situated on the borders of the New Forest, provides residential care and training for people with a mental handicap. The organisation is well staffed and based on the "core and cluster", principle. There are three satellite family group Homes in Bournemouth, a central Home and Training Unit in Ringwood, with a cottage nearby used for training towards independent living.

Due to the retirement of the present Director in March, 1991, the Trustees are inviting applications for this key post. Applicants must hold a social service qualification and have financial and management experience at a senior level in the social services and or the voluntary field.

This is a unique and rewarding post where motivation is of prime importance.

Salary will be commensurate with qualifications and experience, company car or mileage allowance and appropriate relocation expenses.

Enquiries to the Director, The Stable Family Home Trust, Bisterne, Ringwood, Hampshire. Tel: Ringwood (0425) 478043. Closing date for applications - 17th October 1990.

I

ACTION ON SMOKING AND HEALTH (ASH)
DIRECTOR

Smoking kills more than 100,000 people a year in the U.K. and causes vast suffering, disease and disability. It is the nation's largest preventable public health problem.

ASH, a voluntary organisation, is committed to reducing this and receives Department of Health grants and funds from other health related organisations to co-ordinate and lead the fight.

ASH is seeking a new Director (Chief Executive) to replace David Simpson who has a new post as Director of the International Agency on Tobacco and Health. The appointee will have policy analysis and communication skills, and the ability to manage programmes and provide leadership to a small enthusiastic, committed team.

Salary negotiable - but not less than £25,000.

Further information about ASH and the post of Director is available from the Honorary Secretary, Dr Noel Olsen, at 21 Pond Street, London NW3 2PN (071-794 0431 x 2712). Applications in the form of a CV, should be received by 19th October.

Which advertisement is looking for someone who

1. can give advice about looking after historical sites?

2. wants to work with people who cannot cope with everyday life?

3. is a trained lawyer?

4. would welcome the chance of learning management skills?

5. can help a variety of organisations with similar aims to work together?

6. will work in London for one year?

7. will raise money to send people abroad to work?

Which advertisement is for a job which

8. involves passing on specialist knowledge to fellow professionals?

9. excludes some people on account of nationality?

10. is available because the current holder is retiring?

Which advertisement

11. implies that it will check applicants' references?

12. seeks to recruit for a range of jobs?

13. implies that applicants will be tested?

14. suggests that the previous holder will still be working in a related field?

SECOND TEXT: QUESTIONS 15–19

*Read the following article from a weekend newspaper and answer questions
15–19 by choosing A, B, C or D.*

IT IS HARD to love ants.
Spiders and scorpions excepted, they are probably our least favourite insect. They give no honey; they do not brighten the air or chirp in hedgerows. Ants are small and dark and silent and live underground where they cannot be seen. They are venomous and they bite. They teem and swarm, moving *en masse*, like robots, in cryptic legions. And they are ugly; their huge heads and tiny waists make their bodies seem like grotesque, anorexic versions of our own. The industry of ants is a constant reproach to us; their most surprising feature, their social organisation, seems sinister and totalitarian. Only our luck in being several thousand times as big keeps us safe from them.

And ants, needless to say, do not love us. They hardly even notice us. This is hard to take. They challenge our anthropocentrism. For them, it seems we are not very important. And that is the truth of the matter. Ants are the most successful organisms in evolutionary history: there are over 8,000 species, distributed everywhere on Earth except the polar regions. In Peru, 43 different kinds of ant have been recorded in a single tree. Compared to this, primates are just a flash in the pan. Ants antedate us and will undoubtedly outlast us. There are a million times more of them: 10 million billion, it has been estimated, alive at any one time – a quarter of a million for every acre of land on the Earth's surface.

The greatest number of ant species, and the most spectacular, are to be found in tropical rainforests and savannahs. It is a common but disconcerting ex-

perience in such places to witness an invasion of driver ants, a predatory tribe that hunts at night as well as in the day. Driver ants move in columns a foot or so in width and a hundred yards in length, each composed of millions of individual ants. Waking up in the darkness with a marauding column in your tent, it seems as though a thick black oiled rope is running over your bed, over you, across the wall and out again: an endless skein of insects, running along each other's backs, antennae and mandibles threateningly erect. A column of driver ants will attack lizards, snakes, rodents, anything in its path. If you happen to be dead, the ants will eat you, too; if you are not, they will just bite you. With their preposterously over-developed jaws, individuals of the soldier castes that form the flank of the column can scissor human flesh with ease. These are the rottweilers of the myrmecological world.

Ants can eat us, but we cannot eat them with any pleasure. Unlike termites (which have a rich oily taste something like pork scratchings), ants, with a tough outer layer of chitin and a nasty whiff of formic acid in their body

tissues, are generally undigestible, except by other ants. Even anteaters prefer termites. Ants, furthermore, are resistant to hard radiation and, in the case of some species, industrial pollution; some can live in deserts; some can float; some can slow their metabolism down and survive under water for days on end.

Why are ants so successful? Instead of the endless competition of human societies, where social hierarchies are continually demolished and rebuilt, ants have the division of labour written into their physiology. The ant colony is an almost exclusively female society, with the males remaining in the nest only until the time of their fatal nuptial flight. Like other social insects, males mate once and die. Workers, wingless non-reproductive females, are physically differentiated from birth, bred for toil and sterility.

Ants waste no time and do not play. They fight – in defence of the colony, the breeding unit – but they do not have civil wars or revolutions. The survival and expansion of the colony is the only aim of its members. The colony, in fact, can be thought of as a single diffuse being, a creature with 100,000 mouths.

Visual material for paper 5 Phase B

1A

2E

1B

2F

C2

1C

1D

1E

1F

1G

1H

2A

2B

2C

2D

3A

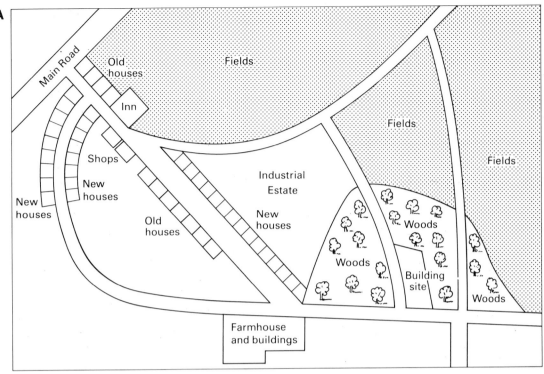

Main Road

Old houses

Fields

Inn

Shops

New houses

New houses

Old houses

Industrial Estate

New houses

Fields

Fields

Woods

Woods

Building site

Woods

Farmhouse and buildings

4A

3B

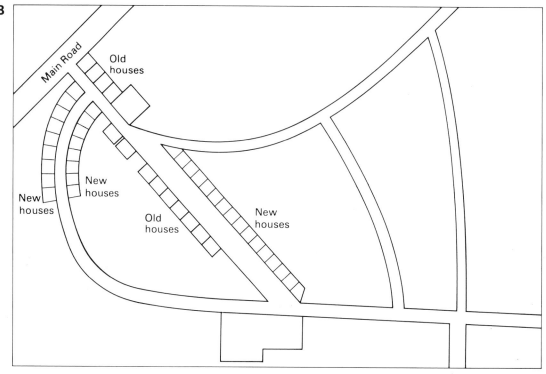

Main Road

Old houses

New houses

New houses

Old houses

New houses

4B

3C

3D

3E

3F

4C

4D

4E

4F

4G

4H

4I

4J

4K

4L

4M

4N

15. The author feels that the fact that ants are always working
    A   makes humans feel lucky.
    B   makes humans feel guilty.
    C   makes them appear sinister.
    D   makes them hard to love.

16. Apart from their great numbers, why does the writer call ants 'the most successful organisms'?
    A   They do not need to take account of human beings.
    B   They challenge mankind's view that humans are the most important life form.
    C   There are thousands of them in every land on Earth.
    D   They existed before humans and will exist after we have gone.

17. How does the writer describe the feelings of someone who observes the approach of driver ants?
    A   frightened
    B   distressed
    C   insecure
    D   uneasy

18. What creatures are best equipped to digest ants?
    A   certain humans
    B   anteaters
    C   other ants
    D   termites

19. How does the writer account for the success of ants?
    A   The majority of ants are females and can only work.
    B   Ants cannot exist as individuals.
    C   There is no hierarchy within a colony.
    D   Ants work only for the good of their colony.

THIRD TEXT: QUESTIONS 20–28

Look at the page entitled 'The Month Ahead'. Choose which of the telephone numbers from the box below you should phone if you are interested in each of the following and mark A–J to show your answer.

20. pictures by Glasgow artists ☐

21. pictures of homes in Glasgow ☐

22. personal possessions of royalty ☐

23. items made to commemorate kings and queens ☐

24. general art history ☐

25. learning how to preserve things dug up by archaeologists ☐

26. learning ancient craft techniques ☐

27. visiting famous archaeological sites ☐

28. seeing things discovered in the course of new building work ☐

A	071 938 8638
B	031 225 7534
C	041 221 7030
D	0736 757575
E	0904 611944
F	071 584 9161
G	081 806 4325
H	071 253 6644
I	041 357 3929
J	0243 63301

THE MONTH AHEAD

August 6th: The History of Fine and Decorative Arts in the West, The Victoria and Albert Museum's Summer Course, which aims to give participants a broad outline of the fine and decorative arts in the west from the Classical period until the 1970s. Details from the museum's education department, South Kensington, London SW7 2RL (071 938 8638).

7th: Gertrude Jekyll, a lecture by Judith Tankard on the Edwardian gardener, subtitled 'A Vision of Garden and Wood'. Details from the Tradescant Trust, Museum of Garden History, St Mary-at-Lambeth, Lambeth Palace Road, London SE1 7JU (071 261 1891).

10th: The Landscape of Kenwood, an exhibition at Kenwood House which looks at the park surrounding the house; Humphrey Repton's late eighteenth-century design still survives, but is under threat from a combination of over-use and modern land management techniques, so the exhibition looks at past, present and future. Details from The Iveagh Bequest, Kenwood, Hampstead Lane, London NW3 (081 348 1286).

Dynasty, The Royal House of Scotland, is a new permanent exhibition organised by the Royal Museum of Scotland and the Scottish National Portrait Gallery. For twelve generations the Stewarts ruled Scotland – from Robert the Bruce to Queen Anne. As well as portraits, the exhibition will include objects associated with the individuals and their daily lives. Details from the museum, 1 Queen Street, Edinburgh (031 225 7534).

15th: Tenements and Towers, a chronicle of 100 years of housing in Glasgow through photographs owned by the Royal Commission on the Ancient and Historical Monuments of Scotland from the model tenement buildings of the late nineteenth century through world wars, depression, and the gradual improvements of the late twentieth century. Details from the Mitchell Library, North Street, Glasgow 3 (041 221 7030).

17th: Lindisfarne and the Early Church, a four-day tour around Northumberland, Yorkshire and Durham, the centre for the early spread of Christianity in Northern Britain. Places visited include Monkwearmouth and Jarrow, Durham Cathedral and other smaller churches in the region. Details from Past Times Tours, Guildford House, Hayle, Cornwall TR27 6PT (0736 757575).

18th: A National Archaeologists Day for young people is being organised by The Young Archaeologists Club. Ten archaeological sites across the country are providing a day of activities such as site tours, prehistoric pot firing and training excavation for all the family. Information from Karen McMahon at the club, Clifford Chambers, 4 Clifford Street, York YO1 1RD (0904 611944).

20th: Long To Reign Over Us, a four-day exhibition, prior to its sale, at Bonhams of the collection of more than 400 pieces of china made as souvenirs of royalty and royal occasions – from William and Mary delftware to items from the present day – all collected by Herbert Ward. Details from Bonhams, Montpelier Street, SW7 (071 584 9161).

24th: Manners, Morals and Mirrors, a three-day course on the paintings of everyday life in seventeenth-century Holland which, beneath their realistic veneer, carry moralising messages in symbolic images. Details from the University of Cambridge Board of Extra-Mural Studies, Madingley Hall, Madingley, Cambridge CB3 8AQ (0954 210636).

Current Archaeology in Southern Britain, a four-day tour which visits the leading excavation sites in the region. Details from Citisights, 213 Brooke Road, London E5 8AB (081 806 4325).

Clerkenwell's Hidden Heritage, the closing date of an exhibition organised jointly by the Museum of London and the Museum of the Order of St John. Recent redevelopments in the area have enabled archaeologists to examine many sites in the area and much new information has been acquired as well as a variety of finds made. Details from the Museum of the Order of St John, St John's Square, Clerkenwell, London EC1M 4DA (071 253 6644).

24th: Glasgow Girls examines the role of women in Glasgow's cultural renaissance between 1880 and 1920 when the 'Glasgow Style' was created. The exhibition will show some 200 items of fine and decorative art which illustrate the contribution of the Glasgow girls. Details from Kelvingrove Art Gallery (041 357 3929).

Field Archaeology is a four-day course at West Dean College, which includes practical excavation at the Batten Hanger Roman villa on the West Dean estate, and also work at the Chichester conservation laboratory. Details from West Dean College, West Dean, Chichester, West Sussex (0243 63301).

FOURTH TEXT: QUESTIONS 29–35

Read this passage about cave dwellers and answer questions 29–35 by choosing A, B, C or D.

The woman next door is a troglodyte

In France cave dwellers are making a comeback. **Ian Harding** looks at some of the advantages of a home hewn from the rock.

THE traditional image of cave dwellers is probably ape-like creatures clad in skimpy animal skins, complete with clubs and matted hair and chewing unidentifiable bones. But in the region around Saumur, living in caves is making a comeback. Not that it ever completely disappeared.

In a region famous for its wine production (Anjou), it is hardly surprising that caves form a part of local life, but it was the nineteenth century quarries cut into the local tuffeau stone which provided an impetus for cave dwellers. Excavating the stone for building purposes left arched caverns, and local inhabitants found that these provided cheap living quarters. If you wanted to extend them, all you had to do was to hack away a bit more of the easily worked rock. Build a wall across the front, with a door and windows and you had a home.

'It's possible to drive through this area without seeing it properly because so much is underground,' says Michel Renou, director of a recently opened study centre at Doue La Fontaine.

Until recently many cave houses were used for storage, for maturing wine and for growing mushrooms rather than for habitation, but now there is a definite trend back to cave dwelling. Caves are proving particularly popular with painters, sculptors and craft workers. There is even a building firm that specialises in restoring and making safe disused cave houses.

Bernard Foyer, once an electronics executive, moved to a cave this summer, selling his conventional home. 'It's more tranquil,' he explains. 'It suits my state of mind: I like to be left alone in my cave.' He claims that the authorities pay little attention to cave dwellers and, knowing that they often have small incomes, the tax collectors by and large leave them be.

'And they're a lot cheaper to buy than any normal house,' says Mr Foyer. 'I bought my first cave 15 years ago. It had five rooms, a lot of storage space and cost me 1,000 francs [about £100].'

Mr Foyer's latest cave cost him 20,000 frs two years ago. What is it like? You approach the new Foyer residence through a gate, down a steep slope and then into a circular courtyard open to the sky, about 30 feet below the surrounding land. From the road it is invisible. All around the courtyard are little doors and windows set into the rock. Behind them are large, high rooms, some with fireplaces and all connected by passageways. It is light, dry and airy.

Across the road is Mr Foyer's troglodyte neighbour, Mrs Saumorou. She has never lived anywhere but in caves, moving from that of her parents when she married. Her cave consists of one big bed-sitting room, and she sits in front of the log fire, carefully chopping up vegetables for her salad lunches.

'I'm 71,' she says, 'and I don't leave my cave very much now.' The local commune tried to get her to accept a modern apartment in a special development of old people's housing, but 'I told them no,' says Mrs Saumorou. 'This cave is *chez moi*. I would rather die here, in my bed.' She points to an ancient wooden construction in a part of the room covered – wall and ceiling – in patterned wallpaper. The floor is smooth and flat through years of use.

Twenty miles north on the banks of the Loire, we ascend a steep track with views across the river. Two hundred feet below the track, we come across a young couple who bought a cave for 80,000 frs two years ago. In front, there is a small fenced terrace where their small son rides his tricycle, parked outside the kitchen door. 'Caves with a view like this cost more to buy,' says the reserved owner, who runs a cave café nearby. The cave, which cost £8,000, has a flush toilet connected to a septic tank, but no kitchen.

What guidance can anyone offer for those who want to escape convention and live in a cave? 'Aeration,' says Bernard Foyer. 'That is the most important rule; aeration and how you might put in a chimney. The nature of the rock around here is such, however, that the land drains easily and so the caves are rarely damp.'

But it is very important to own the land immediately above your cave. If you don't, the local farmer may decide to plough it, or to remove vegetation which can cause cracks and unstable ceilings. 'And,' Mr Foyer adds, 'if the land is yours, you can grow vegetables around your chimney pot and drop them straight down the chimney into the cooking pot on the stove or fire below.'

There are sound ecological reasons for living below ground. Caves maintain a steady, moderate temperature and so require little in the way of heating. Nor do they occupy valuable agricultural land.

But, as all the owners around Saumur seem to agree, the most compelling reason for choosing to live in a cave is to be found somewhere deep in blood or memory. Warm, cosy, safe, private: caves appeal to our primitive instincts and continue to provide perfectly acceptable homes, free from the guiding hand of architect, speculator or local authority.

---

29. What has the writer found in Saumur?
    A traces of prehistoric cave dwellers
    B caves inhabited since prehistoric times
    C people who dress in animal skins
    D people who choose to live in caves

30. How did cave dwelling start in this region?
    A It is an ancient tradition.
    B The wine producers lived near their stores.
    C Local people moved into holes made when rock was cut.
    D Persecution made it necessary for people to live secretly.

31. Why did Bernard Foyer move to a cave?
    A He wanted to live among artists and craft workers.
    B He wanted somewhere peaceful to live.
    C He was short of money.
    D He wanted to avoid paying taxes.

32. What is unusual about Mrs Saumorou?
    A She has lived in caves all her life.
    B She was married in a cave.
    C She has never been out of her cave.
    D She has decorated her cave with wallpaper.

33. What should be considered most carefully when planning a cave home?
    A drainage
    B heating
    C ventilation
    D lighting

34. Why should the cave dweller own the land above the cave?
    A The weight of heavy farm machinery may cause structural problems.
    B Roots may grow down into the cave through cracks.
    C Change of land use may damage the cave below.
    D Vandals may drop things down the chimney.

35. Why does the writer believe people want to live in caves?
    A They are idealists.
    B They want to escape bureaucratic constraints.
    C They need somewhere very cheap.
    D They are obeying an instinctive urge.

PAPER 2   WRITING   (2 hours)

Answer section A and section B.

SECTION A

A short time ago you spent a holiday with some cousins who live in the USA. One day, the mother and daughter (Kay and Kari) took you for a drive and the car was involved in an accident. Fortunately no-one was seriously injured, but your cousins' car was badly damaged. Today you received this note from your cousin, with the newspaper cutting enclosed:

> How are you? We're all fine and Mom and Dad send you love and want to know when you'll be over here again. Thanks for the photos – we all had a good laugh over them.
>
> The reason I'm writing again so soon is to send you this cutting. Can you believe it? The guy must be crazy! Anybody could see he just pulled out in front of us without looking. Now he wants to involve us in all sorts of hassle, lawyer's fees, etc – presumably just to keep his insurance premiums down. Anyway, would you do us a great favor? Write to his insurers, tell them the correct facts, explain who you are, etc. The more people tell our side of the story the better obviously, and yours might carry extra weight if you've taken the trouble to write from abroad. We'd be most grateful, specially Dad, who's worried because I was driving - at the ripe old age of 19 - he thinks the insurers might be more inclined to think it was my fault because of my age, when we all know it was Mr Lee's. He, of course, hasn't really got a clue who was doing what, as you see from the cutting.
>
> Send the letter to me and I'll pass it on. Just address it "To whom it may concern".
>
> Thanks very much. Take care of yourself. Give our love to your parents.
>
> Love from,
>
> Kari.

Senior Citizen Takes On Insurance Giant

In an unusual move in an insurance case, senior citizen Barry Lee, 67, yesterday announced that he was prepared to go to court to defend his story.

Last month, Mr Lee, a retired optometrist, was involved in an accident with the Turner family. Says Mr Lee, 'I was turning from the Blossomville road onto the highway, having checked carefully that it was clear, when a car, driven very fast by a middle-aged woman, came round the bend and went into the front of me. It's a miracle that no one was seriously injured.'

Mr Lee has refused to accept liability, and points out that the only witnesses were 'a couple of passengers, one of them a very young girl, neither of whom seemed to have any idea what was going on'. He also states that his car was the only one which sustained serious damage and suggests that this may be the reason why the Turner family refuse to admit any responsibility.

Using the information contained in the note and the newspaper cutting, write:

1. An account of the accident as requested by Kari (approximately 200 words).

2. Your covering note to Kari (approximately 50 words).

You may invent extra details if you wish, *provided* that your account remains consistent with Kari's version of events.

SECTION B

*Choose **one** of the following tasks. Your answer should follow exactly the instructions given. You are advised to write approximately 250 words.*

1. You see the following advertisement and decide to answer it:

THE ENGLISH SPEAKERS' EXCHANGE

☆ Spend up to one month in the country of your choice with an English-speaking family or individuals who share your interests, then let them participate in your home and professional life on the same terms.

☆ If you are 16-plus, whether studying or pursuing a career and would like to take part in an exchange, either on an individual or family basis, please write to us, giving the following information:

- your home address, details of the accommodation, description of your family etc.
- what sort of people you would like to meet on your exchange
- which parts of the world you'd like to visit
- the number of people involved (family or other group, individual etc.)

Please note: we do not cater for under-16s, except as members of family groups.

ESE, PO BOX 1543, EDINBURGH, SCOTLAND

---

2. Some overseas visitors will shortly arrive at the institution where you work (or study). You have been asked to write an account, in English, of the daily routine, in particular describing any routines or habits which may be unfamiliar to foreigners.

3. Write a contribution for your college's English language newsletter, describing ways in which attitudes to the environment have changed *in your region* over the past twenty years.

4. You recently borrowed something (car, radio, word processor, etc.) from a colleague. Unfortunately, it has been damaged. Write a letter of apology, explaining what happened and saying how you propose to put matters right.

PAPER 3   ENGLISH IN USE   (1 hour 30 minutes)

SECTION A

1   *Read the extract below and circle the letter next to the word which best fits each space. The first answer has been given as an example.*

The point at which physical decline with age begins adversely to affect a driver's capability has not yet been thoroughly studied. A survey of more than 3,000 road accidents in Michigan ...*involving*... drivers aged over 55 showed that in eight out of ten (1)............................ it was a driver over the age of 71 who had (2)............................ a collision by failing to yield, turning carelessly or changing lanes.

Older drivers are obviously more (3)............................ to injury in vehicle crashes, as well as being a potential higher (4)............................ through their own driving (5).............................

Reaction (6)............................ in an emergency involves many different physical (7)............................ such as the production of the nerve impulse, perception of the signal, (8)............................ of response and transmission to the muscles.

Some of these (9)............................ more than others with age, but the overall effect increases the time it takes to respond for more (10)............................ drivers.

Part of the ageing process, however, does include the (11)............................ of experience, often in the subconscious, which triggers (12)............................ danger warnings than in younger drivers who have not experienced similar situations.

This (13)............................ of judgement heightens the perception of risk and often (14)............................ older drivers to avoid a situation which might then (15)............................ them to the test.

	A	B	C	D
	A reflecting	Ⓑ involving	C excluding	D asking
1.	A users	B points	C cases	D attempts
2.	A avoided	B prevented	C caused	D activated
3.	A likely	B susceptible	C possible	D common
4.	A degree	B chance	C factor	D risk
5.	A practice	B activity	C experience	D behaviour
6.	A period	B time	C process	D system
7.	A events	B parts	C factors	D forms
8.	A choice	B suggestion	C section	D preference
9.	A improve	B deteriorate	C reduce	D increase
10.	A mature	B ancient	C older	D elderly
11.	A collection	B addition	C storage	D summary

12. A sooner   B earlier   C former   D later
13. A lack   B maturity   C absence   D strength
14. A follows   B progresses   C leads   D pulls
15. A fix   B force   C enable   D put

2   *Complete the following extract from an article about hammocks by writing the missing words in the spaces provided. Use only **one** word in each space. The first answer has been given as an example.*

There are warm tropical regions all over the globe, but only the Indians of the South American rain forests have adopted the habit of sleeping in the air. Long ......*before*...... they made their painful acquaintance with Europeans, they had invented something that was unique (1)............................ earth: the hammock.

Nobody (2)............................ knows who first had the felicitous idea of (3)............................ sleeping in the air the symbol of untroubled respose. The Indians see the hammock as a 'gift of heaven', (4)............................ bestowed on them in mythical times.

In it the Indians pass (5)............................ oppressive noon hours dozing or chatting. Swinging it (6)............................ and fro creates a cooling breath of air and keeps (7)............................ insects. (8)............................ work and play in hammocks, are born and die (9).............................

Suspended between heaven and earth, a hammock is dry (10)............................ the soil is damp and is safe (11)............................ most vermin.

Hammocks have the advantage over beds in that they are easy to transport and take (12)............................ very little space when they have (13)............................ rolled up. Indians (14)............................ go on a journey without their hammocks, not (15)............................ to their plantations.

SECTION B

3   *In the extract below from an article about the London Underground map there are incorrectly spelt words in most lines. Write the word but spell it correctly in the space provided or, if you think the line is correct, put a tick (√). Two of the lines have been done for you.*

The London Underground map is a designe classic.		*design*
They keep a copy in the New York Musuem of Modern	1.	....
Art. One of the century's most famous images, it is	2.	....
as much a worldwide symbole of London as Big	3.	....
Ben and Beefeaters. But it only came about because		√
a young enginering draughtsman living in High Barnet	4.	....
was laid of and began sketching a map to fill the time.	5.	....
At first 29-year-old Harry Beck's design was rejected as to	6.	....
revolutionary by London Transport. Uged on by friends,	7.	....
he tried again. This time his map was grugingly accepted	8.	....
and in 1933 five hundred were printed in a trail run. It was	9.	....
an imediate success; for the first time the travelling	10.	....
public could see the Tube system as a hole and could	11.	....
work out how to get around London at a glance.	12.	....
Before Beck, maps were a litteral representation	13.	....
of distance and meandering routes became bewilderingely	14.	....
difficult to follow. Beck realised that it was important to	15.	....
show the order of stations and there connections.	16.	....
Clarity, not geography, was what counted.	17.	....

4 *Read the following informal note you have received from a colleague. Using the information given, complete the formal announcement below by writing the missing words in the spaces provided. The first answer has been given as an example. You should use only* **one or two words** *in each space.*

I've just had a note from the director and got details about the conference in Bologna. It's a three day affair and the general theme will be the teaching of modern languages. The first day will begin with someone- Professor Spinsterson, I think — talking about new ideas in teaching. They were going to have that new professor from America - Emandsan? - but he can't make it.

After this there will be a chance to get into groups and they are probably going to show us some audio-visual aids that have been developed recently.

The next couple of days there are going to be various talks from teachers of Italian and Spanish and the whole thing is going to be rounded off with a debate about the need for language teaching in the primary school.

Apparently any two of us in this department can go. Do you fancy it?

The .... conference in Bologna on	*three-day*
(1) .... teaching techniques will be	1. ....
(2) .... by Professor Spinsterson.	2. ....
He will give the (3) .... session on	3. ....
new (4) .... to language teaching. He	4. ....
will (5) .... Eric Edmonson	5. ....
who unfortunately is unable (6)	6. ....
This will be (7) .... a half-day session on	7. ....
(8) .... audio-visual aids. The following two	8. ....
days will (9) .... Italian and Spanish teachers	9. ....
(10) .... The conference (11)	10. ....
with a discussion entitled (12)	11. ....
be teaching languages in the primary school?	12. ....
There are (13) .... available to members of the	
department staff.	
	13. ....

SECTION C

5 *Read through the following text and then choose the best phrase or sentence, given below, to fill each of the gaps. Write one letter (A–O) in each of the numbered gaps. Some of the suggested answers do not fit at all.*

The most alarming thing about the food scene at the moment is the doubt in the minds of many about the safety of some of our most widely used products. Take aspartame, the sugar substitute. In the United States, as much as $100 million has been spent (1)............................ advertising it. Aspartame, (2)............................, is found in practically every low-calorie soft drink.

   But how safe is it? For quite a while, there has been doubt surrounding the research (3)............................ to prove the safety of NutraSweet. The task force (4)............................ to approve NutraSweet (5)............................ when it felt it couldn't rely on the integrity of the basic idea the firm had submitted.

   Last July, Dr Erik Millstone of the University of Sussex submitted a dossier to the Department of Health (6)............................ in the approval of aspartame in the United States (7)............................ that three of the 14 members of the Committee on Toxicity in this country (8)............................ with the artificial sweetener industry.

   I've been reading a book (9)............................ who claims that aspartame can cause headaches, convulsions, memory loss and diarrhoea. He has collected (10)............................ that has convinced him that aspartame is not as safe as the makers claim. As it is now used in some 1,200 products, (11)............................ are virtually unlimited.

A the chances of avoiding aspartame
B and he finds it strange
C as the makers claim
D by an American doctor
E ran into difficulties
F describing misuse of funds
G a mass of anecdotal evidence
H in some years
I set up by the US Food and Drug Administration
J alleging criminal fraud
K are attached
L the opportunities for ingesting aspartame
M under its brand name NutraSweet
N that was conducted
O have financial links

6 *You have had an accident in your car and you are going to make an insurance claim. As you will have to include a short description of what happened on the claim form, you make the few notes given below. Expand these notes into a full description of what took place. You must use all the words in the notes but not necessarily in the same order and you may add words and change the form of the words where necessary. Look carefully at the example which has been done for you.*

a) Friday evening / driving home / 6 o'clock

b) traffic heavy / getting dark / joined line of stationary cars / Victoria Avenue

c) obviously hold-up / probably traffic light stuck

d) suddenly loud bang / back my car / forwards and upwards

e) shocked / turned / saw driver behind / getting out

f) first words / sorry, all right? / foot slipped brake

g) car mess / bonnet hit car in front / serious dent

h) car behind / boot pushed in

i) do nothing / sit, wait police / none move

a)	It was Friday evening and I was driving home about 6 o'clock.
b)	
c)	
d)	
e)	
f)	
g)	
h)	
i)	

PAPER 4   LISTENING   (45 minutes)

Answer all questions.

SECTION A

You will hear someone giving advice on creating a wildlife garden which will encourage wild animals and birds to visit. For questions 1–8 tick those pictures which show what you should do and put a cross against those which are not mentioned or are not suggested. Listen carefully. You will hear the piece twice.

Picture 1

Picture 2

Picture 3

Picture 4

Picture 5

Picture 6

⟫→

Picture 7 ☐   Picture 8 ☐

SECTION B

You will hear someone explaining how to get to the English Language faculty on a university campus. On the map, complete the labels 9–18 showing various places and objects which he mentions. Listen carefully as you will hear this piece once only.

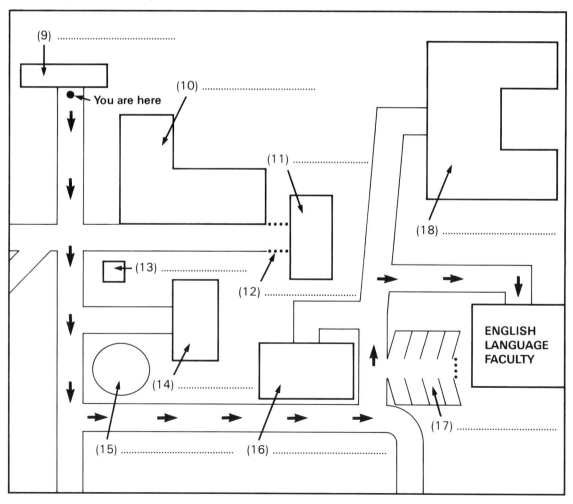

SECTION C

Listen to Richard Ramsay talking about how he invented and marketed a case for skis. Look at questions 19–24 and tick the best answer A, B, C or D. You will hear the interview twice.

19. The main purpose of the Ski tube is to
    A transport skis to the airport.
    B reduce the cost of maintaining skis.
    C make the skis easy to carry.
    D allow skis to be carried on buses and coaches.

20. The design of the tube had to take into account
    A the varying length of skis.
    B the importance of fitting good ski-brakes.
    C the weight of the skis.
    D the need for a removable handle.

21. In what way was ICI able to help the designer?
    A They were able to give him sound financial advice.
    B They suggested he made the tubes from a particular material.
    C They agreed to keep his design a secret.
    D They offered to back his project in return for supplying the raw material.

22. What was Ramsay's main concern?
    A finding someone to market his invention for him
    B coming up with enough money to finance his project
    C fighting a large company's takeover bid
    D finding people who would want to buy his product

23. What was Ramsay's attitude towards being funded by someone else?
    A He was glad of their managerial skills.
    B He was upset at having to use outside funding.
    C He was happy as long as he was still in control.
    D He found it difficult to relate to them on a personal level.

24. What has been the biggest problem to have faced Ramsay?
    A breaking into a market which is not traditionally a British interest
    B convincing people he has a quality product to sell
    C translating advertisements into the appropriate European language
    D discussing business deals with people who don't speak English

SECTION D

You will hear various people talking. There are five extracts which are not related in any way except that everyone is talking about being young. You will hear the people twice.

Task 1

For questions 25–29 look at the topics below labelled A–H. As you listen, put the topics in the order in which you hear them by completing the boxes 25–29 with the appropriate letter. Three topics will not be used.

A   what young people look like

B   the problems of bringing up children

C   young people being a nuisance

D   why children are fortunate

E   things that attract young people

F   the difficulties of being young today

G   how young children can be stimulating company

H   the best years of your life

Topic 1	25.	
Topic 2	26.	
Topic 3	27.	
Topic 4	28.	
Topic 5	29.	

Task 2

For questions 30–34 look at the types of people listed below labelled A–H. As you listen, decide in what order you hear each person speak and complete the boxes 30–34 with the appropriate letter. Three people will not be used.

A   a teacher

B   a policeman

C   a teenager

D   a politician

E   an advertising consultant

F   a parent

G   a doctor

H   an old lady

30.	
31.	
32.	
33.	
34.	

PAPER 5   SPEAKING   (15 minutes)

PHASE A

The examiners will introduce themselves to you and then invite you to talk about yourself.

PHASE B1

Candidate A

The examiner will ask your partner to describe a village to you. You must mark your plan so that it is complete. After one minute you will be able to compare your plans.

Candidate B

The examiner will ask you to describe a village to your partner using your plan, so that s/he can add some features which are missing from his/her plan. You will be able to compare your plans at the end of one minute.

PHASE B2

Candidate A

The examiner will ask your partner to describe a picture to you. At the end of one minute the examiner will ask you to say which picture your partner has described.

Candidate B

The examiner will ask you to describe a picture to your partner. At the end of one minute your partner will be asked to say which picture you have described.

PHASE C

Candidates A and B

The examiner will ask you and your partner to have a discussion about three topics. For each one, you must reach agreement or agree to differ. At the end of four minutes you will be asked to report your decision to the examiners.

Discuss each of the topics below and say whether you believe they have, on the whole, improved or deteriorated over the past 50 years.
- educational standards
- food production methods
- urban transport systems

PHASE D

The examiners will join your discussion and you will be asked more
questions relating to the previous task.

Practice Test 4

PAPER 1 READING (1 hour)

Answer all questions.

FIRST TEXT: QUESTIONS 1–17

Read this article from a local business paper and answer the questions which follow.

When the answer is to question . . .

*Dr Jean Hammond, of Management Dynamics,
deals with issues she encounters
during the course of her work.*

RECENTLY I found myself (informally) counselling a senior manager who was bewildered and furious in equal proportions.

The cause? He had done something benevolent for the people in his division only to have it blow up in his face in an apparently unpredictable way. His entirely predictable reaction was 'The ungrateful so-and-so's. Never again'.

It is easy to empathise with the injured party, but why do things go wrong in this way? This week I have chosen two case histories to illustrate the problem, and have then gone on to see what generalisations are possible so that we can avoid 'doing the right thing wrong'.

The first case concerns the managing director in a client company who booked two of his middle managers on a team building seminar.

This was a prestigious event being led by a sought-after consultant with an international reputation and held in the opulence of a posh London hotel. The attendance fee was not much under £500 apiece, so the direct cost was over £1000, plus the opportunity cost of their time.

He had singled them out because they were both keen on and normally receptive to the idea of self development, they were hard workers and high flyers, and he wanted to send a clear message to them about how pleased he was with their performance.

Warm

When he handed over their tickets, he received a response that could generously be described as luke warm, and the only feedback he had from them after the event was that it had been 'all right'.

When he probed further, he discovered simmering resentment which could be paraphrased as 'We head up two of the best and smoothest functioning teams in the place. Why pick on us? What have we done wrong?' Hardly able to credit such ingratitude our man went off in a huff and with the silent resolve to be less generous in the future.

Gesture

The second example, from the States, concerns the Berkshire Foundry where they had a profitable year. The board wan-

ted to make a gesture of appreciation and after some brain storming decided that they would air-condition the refectory.

In the production areas the ambient temperature was 40 degrees centigrade or more, and it was felt that being able to retreat into a cool environment over lunch time would be a real treat. The work was duly carried out.

A year later profits were once again good, and once again the board found itself wondering how it might reward productivity. Someone pointed out that there had been no follow-up study of the air-conditioning of the refectory. Had the gesture been appreciated? Had it perhaps even contributed to the excellent productivity? Since the answers to these questions were not known, the chairman asked the personnel director to undertake an internal survey to establish reaction to the air-conditioning of the refectory.

The majority response to his survey was 'I didn't know that it was air-conditioned'. Some 20% of the sample revealed that they never ate there. A similar number complained 'If management can chuck money around like this they should be paying us more'. Others took the line 'Why isn't the whole plant air-conditioned?'

No more than 5% of the sample gave it a stamp of approval if 'It's OK' can be called that.

This was clearly not the outcome the board had been expecting, nor was it one that was likely to fire them with enthusiasm for their next benevolent gesture.

Wrong

Despite the many differences that must apply, the two cases have much in common. What went wrong?

A major part of the answer is

'No one asked me'. It is not a question of pandering to egalitarianism. It is common sense.

This approach is no more than a special case of the general principle: Where possible, involve everyone who is going to be affected by a decision.

We operate in an age where consultation is, or should be, part of the fabric of work. These cases show that no matter how unfair it seems, it is a terrible mistake to think that it can be bypassed just because we are doing something 'nice'.

For questions 1–6 choose one of the feelings A–I in Box 2 to match each of the people in Box 1. No option in Box 2 is used more than once.

1

1. The manager recently counselled by the writer

2. The two middle managers on receiving their tickets for the seminar

3. The two middle managers being given an opportunity to develop their potential in normal circumstances

4. The managing director decided to send his managers to the seminar to show he

5. On being questioned after the seminar the two middle managers revealed that they

6. On learning of his employees' reaction to having been to the seminar the managing director

was / were

2

A embarrassed.

B puzzled and angry.

C enthusiastic.

D offended.

E distressed.

F grateful.

G sulky.

H cool.

I outraged.

For questions 7–11 choose one of the people / groups A–G in Box 4 to match
the phrase from the text in Box 3. No option in Box 4 is used more than once.

4

A   the board at Berkshire Foundry.

B   the manager recently counselled
      by the writer.

3

7.   'the injured party'

8.   'a sought-after consultant'

9.   'high flyers'

10.   'our man'

11.   'the sample'

means

C   middle managers.

D   workers at Berkshire Foundry.

E   the personnel director.

F   the leader of the team building
      seminar.

G   the managing director.

For questions 12 and 13 choose one of the feelings A–D in Box 6 to match
each group of people in Box 5. No option in Box 6 is used more than once.

5

12.   The workers at the Berkshire Foundry on
      being informed that the refectory had been
      air-conditioned

13.   The board at the Berkshire Foundry on
      learning the results of the survey

felt

6

A   disappointed.

B   relieved.

C   embarrassed.

D   indifferent.

For questions 14–17 choose one of the definitions A–G in Box 8 to match
each of the phrases from the text in Box 7. No option in Box 8 is used more
than once.

8

A   air-conditioning the refectory.

B   continuing high profits.

C   reaction to the air-conditioning.

7

14.   'gesture of
      appreciation'

15.   'real treat'

16.   'follow-up study'

17.   'stamp of approval'

refers to

D   survey of opinion.

E   getting everyone involved.

F   being in a cool place.

G   carrying out the work.

SECOND TEXT: QUESTIONS 18–23

Read this extract about piano competitions and answer questions 18–23 by choosing A, B, C or D.

Scaling down the bloody combat at the Steinway

Piano competitions attract bad press: but at Santander winning no longer looms so large

IT IS one am and the last competitor in the last round of the Santander Piano Competition is still only halfway through Tchaikovsky's B flat minor concerto, the third account we have heard in two days. Three thousand people, shoe-horned into an auditorium created by the transformation of a handsome Spanish plaza into something like Selfridge's Christmas grotto, fan themselves frantically under the television lights, as heat and tension rise in corresponding leaps. It will be a long night, stretching on until 5.30 am when the judges give their verdict. At 11.30 am the finalists are on duty again, forcing sleep-starved features into brave smiles for the press call.

It is a tough routine – illustrative, you might think, of the familiar arguments against competitions: the blood-sports mentality, the arbitrary nature of the findings (competitions favour 'competition-winners', not 'musicians') and the effect on the participants' lives. Recent history suggests you may be more likely to build an enduring reputation (beyond the round of official engagements that usually come with competition prizes) not by winning but by losing – spectac-ularly and with maximum dissent on the jury, in the way Ivo Pogorolich managed to lose the Chopin competition in Warsaw.

That said, competitions are – especially for pianists – marketplaces in which young performers meet not only their future audience but their future agents and, maybe, record companies. They provide the kick-start with which most high-octane careers are launched. And if the pressures are intense, so are the pressures of the performing world. Music is a fiercely competitive activity.

But pause here for clarification of terms. As Rosalyn Tureck, veteran Bach authority and one of this year's jurors at Santander, told me: 'It's the career that's competitive, not the art. Never confuse them. I don't put competitions down: they do bring talent forward. But if from the age of eight your whole study is geared to the sort of repertory thought desirable for competitions (big, impressive, technically virtuosic) you will never develop as an artist. It will limit your horizons at a time when they need widening, and it will give your performance style, the feeling of a quick feed: a rapid injection with 25,000 units of Vitamin C that makes an instant impression but isn't ultimately very nourishing.'

With such reservations, why was Dr Tureck on the Santander jury? Her answer would be that Santander does succeed in making the competition process more purposeful, less damaging and (not least) more humane than most. 'The letter of invitation summed it up. It said: "These are not the Olympic Games." And that's a big step forward in competition thinking.'

18. What is the purpose of the description in the first paragraph?
    A to demonstrate how tough a music competition may be
    B to shock the reader
    C to persuade the reader that competitions are exciting
    D to show how unusual Santander is

19. Why does the writer refer to the arguments against competitions as 'familiar'?
    A He feels they are taken for granted.
    B He assumes the reader knows them already.
    C He believes they should be debated more publicly.
    D He thinks musicians are insufficiently aware of them.

20. Why is Ivo Pogorolich mentioned?
    A as an example of a 'competition winner', rather than a 'musician'
    B because he realised he would do better in his career if he lost
    C because he made a spectacle of himself when he lost
    D as an example of someone who built a reputation in spite of losing

21. What does the writer find to say in favour of competitions?
    A They offer much-needed cash prizes.
    B They are broadcast to a wide audience.
    C They give a spectacular start to the best musical careers.
    D They allow young musicians to develop friendships.

22. What criticism does Dr Rosalyn Tureck make of competitions?
    A They make young musicians aggressively competitive.
    B They discourage the teaching of a variety of musical styles.
    C They encourage poor teaching techniques.
    D They may damage the health of sensitive young musicians.

23. What did Dr Tureck seek to prove about Santander by quoting from her letter of invitation?
    A that the pressure is less intense
    B that the competitors suffered no physical harm
    C that she was invited to be on the jury
    D that she had the right to comment

THIRD TEXT: QUESTIONS 24–30

Read this article from a newspaper and answer questions 24–30 by choosing A, B, C or D.

Riddle of ancient mariners

AUTUMN is here. Pegasus, Andromeda and Cetus appear – barren, sprawling constellations of stars. Yet the creatures represented by their patterns could not be called dull. According to classical mythology, Cetus is a fierce sea monster, Pegasus a winged horse, Andromeda a princess tied to a rock by the seashore waiting for Cetus to devour her. It prompts the question: why do the constellation patterns usually bear no resemblance to what they supposedly portray?

Time was when the world's different cultures each had their own constellation patterns. North American Indians 'joined up the dots' in a way peculiar to them; the ancient Chinese had myriad tiny constellation patterns, some consisting of just one star; the Aborigines saw the sky as so white with stars that they made patterns out of the places where few stars could be seen.

The patterns we know today are a legacy of the cultures that flourished around the Mediterranean thousands of years ago. But who named the stars, and why?

We first read of our familiar constellations in a poem written by the Greek poet Aratus in 250 BC. Commissioned by the King of Macedonia, *The Phaenomena* celebrates a globe of the stars lost about a century earlier. The globe had belonged to the mathematician Eudoxus, who fortunately left a detailed description of its appearance, which Aratus incorporated into his poem.

The Phaenomena describes the constellations and their relationship to one another in a way that enables one to visualise the appearance of the sky very accurately. It contains many instructions alluding to navigation. One researcher describes the poem as 'a manual for seamen'.

Across the sky there are examples of well-known stories pegged to stars. What better aid to memory could a largely uneducated navigator-sailor have than an association of childhood stories with star patterns in the sky?

Who were the astro-navigators? It is certain that they were not contemporaries of Aratus, or even the earlier Eudoxus; a discovery by a later Greek – Hipparchus – makes that clear. Hipparchus found that the constellations 'slip' relative to the horizon, over timescales of thousands of years. The reason is that the Earth is wobbling in space like a spinning-top – a result of the gravitational pull of the Sun and the Moon on the Earth's equatorial bulge. Over a period of 16,000 years, the Earth's north pole traces out a cone in the sky. This means that the 'celestial pole' (and with it, the Pole Star) and 'celestial equator' are always changing position with respect to the constellations.

The descriptions of the constellations in *The Phaenomena* are all consistent – but not for the time of Aratus, and not for his latitude. It seems that the globe represented the sky as seen from 36 degrees north in about 2800 BC. Evidently, the globe was an artefact from a much earlier civilization – but which?

One possibility is the Egyptians, who flourished at that time. But their astronomical interests lay in timekeeping, not navigation, and their latitude (30 degrees north) is too far south. The Phoenicians used the stars for navigation *and* lived at the correct latitude – but their civilization reached its peak much later than 2800 BC.

The Babylonians – or the Sumero-Akkadians, their forerunners – are a better bet. But they did most of their navigation in the Indian Ocean, where a globe showing the Mediterranean stars would be of little use.

But there was one great Mediterranean civilization – possibly the greatest – that flourished during the second and third millennia BC: the Minoans. Crete's latitude, 36 degrees north, fits exactly that of the globe-makers.

Were the Minoans the globe-makers? We may never know. Much of what we might have learnt about them must have been destroyed in 1450 BC, when the nearby volcanic island of Thira (Santorini) erupted and overwhelmed the eastern part of Crete, wiping out the Minoans.

If they did make star globes with which to navigate the Mediterranean, it is the Minoans whom we can thank for the familiar layout of the constellations, a legacy from almost 5,000 years ago.

24. What prompts the question at the end of the first paragraph?
    A Pegasus, Cetus and Andromeda are dull constellations with exciting names.
    B Pegasus, Cetus and Andromeda have no connection with autumn.
    C Only Pegasus is connected with the sky.
    D Many people find astronomy boring and incomprehensible.

25. Why does the writer mention the North American Indians, ancient Chinese and Aborigines?
    A to demonstrate that ancient Chinese technology was the most advanced
    B to illustrate different ways of describing the stars
    C to prove that southern cultures produce the most original astronomers
    D to show that all cultures study astronomy

26. What was Aratus's source for *The Phaenomena*?
    A the royal house of Macedonia
    B an ancient globe
    C the writings of Eudoxus
    D a lost poem

27. The writer makes the assumption that the seamen of ancient times
    A were very superstitious.
    B made up stories about the stars.
    C loved poetry.
    D had little formal education.

28. Thanks to a discovery made by Hipparchus we know that
    A the positions of the constellations alter over a long period of time.
    B the gravity of the Sun and Moon cause the Earth to bulge at the equator.
    C constellations disappear over a period of 26,000 years.
    D stars change position within constellations.

29. What is puzzling about the descriptions of the constellations in *The Phaenomena*?
    A They are not consistent with those of Eudoxus.
    B They are not correct for 250 BC.
    C They match those on the globe.
    D They show that Aratus did not understand latitude.

30. What does the writer suggest about the Minoans?
    A They were better astronomers than any other ancient civilisation.
    B They sailed from the Mediterranean to other parts of the world.
    C Their view of the stars was used by the Greeks.
    D They used accurate maps of the Mediterranean.

FOURTH TEXT: QUESTIONS 31–38

Read this article and then for questions 31–34 choose the best paragraph from A–E to fill each of the numbered gaps in the text. (There is one extra paragraph which does not belong in any of the gaps.)

Donovan Wilkins is a water diviner. He lives in Cornwall in a village called Chacewater. Sounds like a joke? Well, his talents are far from laughable. With a crude hazel twig that twitches in response to some incomprehensible force, he can do what grown scientists and machines often fail to do, and that is to pinpoint underground water supplies with astonishing accuracy.

It was wet Cornish weather the day I called on him. Dark rain-laden cloud scudded down the valley near Truro; Atlantic moisture dropped from the leaden skies by the bucketful.

31.

So what does a water diviner do, and how does he do it? 'Well, every time I go on a job, it's a journey into the unknown,' he admitted. 'I always work on the basis of "No water – No pay". I'm a bold man, but I have to be.'

32.

'Do you want to believe it?' He looked me in the eye, searching for an honest answer. I gave him one. 'Yes, I do.' He took hold of one arm of the forked hazel twig and gave me the other. We twisted it backwards till the natural springiness in it seemed to bring it alive. Then we walked, very slowly, the stick rock steady. Four paces, five paces. Then, amazingly, the rod flew downward towards the earth. It flicked and it dived.

33.

'Do you want to try it yourself?' he asked. I nodded, still somewhat shaken. 'Remember,' he warned, 'doubt it for one second and it won't work. To your own self be true.' I held on. 'Use all your senses,' he urged me. 'Hear the water in the stream? Well, listen to it. Think water, think water.' I took hold of both arms of the hazel rod and brought it to life with a twist.

A It twisted his wrist as much as it twisted mine. 'I can get really hurt this way,' he told me. 'I can't do it more than a few days a week or the hands get very sore.' He showed me the scars to prove it. With his foot, he marked the spot where the rod had given its unmistakable signal.

B 'Is it harder to find water when it's raining?' I asked, tongue in cheek. 'When you're looking for water 200 feet down, a bit of rain up top doesn't make much difference', he replied.

C 'A few years later, I was cutting a hedge and there was this hazel stick. I just walked across the field with it and away it went, violently. You might say it's magic but to me it's very natural and ordinary.'

D Donovan told me to close my eyes and think. I shuffled forward, very slowly. Nothing for several paces, and then a trembling. A further step, a distinct vibration. Then the rod took charge, twisting and waving, and nothing that I could have done would have held it still. 'Open your eyes,' Donovan said, 'and look down'. I was on exactly the mark where the rod had performed before. Donovan explained that beneath us was an underground stream that fed his pond. I was convinced.

E In the garage are the tools of his trade. 'A stick is a stick is a stick . . . and it isn't,' he declares. 'It's a stick when you pick it up, but pull the fork outwards and it becomes a divining rod.' He grabs hold of a few in quick succession, twists them briefly and judges them to be either good or bad. He picked one up and we went outside. Then followed a most remarkable experience.

34.

I was also surprised, but Donovan said I shouldn't have been. 'You need a natural propensity for it, but I would say it was there in most people. You know when you go into a house and a shiver goes down your spine, and you think "I don't like it here?" Well, it's the same thing – you're dowsing. It's a sixth sense, and what we do is add that sixth sense to the other five.'

For questions 35–38, choose the best answer A, B, C or D.

35. What sounds like a joke?
    A   the fact that Donovan Wilkins lives in Cornwall
    B   the fact that a water diviner lives in a village called Chacewater
    C   the fact that a man called Wilkins describes himself as a water diviner
    D   the fact that a Cornishman claims to be a water diviner

36. How is the stick held while divining?
    A   in two hands, as still as possible
    B   in one hand, as still as possible
    C   in two hands, moving gently from side to side
    D   in one hand, with a slight up and down movement

37. Why was the writer 'somewhat shaken'?
    A   The movement of the stick had injured him.
    B   He had fallen to the ground.
    C   He was startled by what had happened.
    D   His faith had been restored so simply.

38. Donovan believes that most people
    A   believe in water divining.
    B   should try water divining.
    C   despise water divining.
    D   are capable of water divining.

PAPER 2   WRITING   (2 hours)

Answer section A and section B.

SECTION A

While you are working for an international corporation, you receive the following note from a senior colleague who is planning to send his daughter (aged 20) to North America for a few months to study English.

I've seen these two adverts for Eng. lang. courses and think they might be suitable for Sonia — what do you think of them? Can you find out what sort of cities Vancouver and Philadelphia are?

Many thanks

Aziz

STUDY ENGLISH
AT A
WORLD CLASS
UNIVERSITY

THE INTENSIVE ENGLISH LANGUAGE PROGRAMME OF TEMPLE UNIVERSITY PROVIDES:

* 6 levels of instruction from beginner to advanced
* small classes with professional, experienced ESL instructors
* use of the modern, fully equipped language laboratory and computer center
* American conversation partners
* opportunity to enroll in university courses

TEMPLE UNIVERSITY, located in Philadelphia, Pennsylvania is a fully accredited major urban university with an enrollment of approximately 30,000 students. The University is within easy access to New York and Washington, D.C.

For more information contact:

INTENSIVE ENGLISH LANGUAGE PROGRAM
303-N Mitten Hall, Temple University
Philadelphia, PA 19122 U.S.A. (215) 787-7899

THE UNIVERSITY OF BRITISH COLUMBIA
Study English in Vancouver, Canada

The English Language Institute

- a leading Canadian language institute founded in 1969
- accredited by Council of Second Languages of Canada
- part of Canada's second largest university
- in a safe city with a mild climate and spectacular scenery

ENGLISH LANGUAGE INSTITUTE

Year-Round Programs
12 or 6 weeks

- Communication
- Academic Preparation

The Learning Experience

- well qualified, experienced teachers
- students 18 years and older
- programs for individuals and groups
- airport welcome, homestay and dormitory
- cultural and recreational program

Spring & Summer Programs
3–6 weeks

- Residential English
- English for EFL Teachers
- International Business English
- Conversation

Contact: **Marion Torres**
English Language Institute, UBC
5997 Iona Drive, Vancouver, B.C.
Canada V6T 2A4 Tel:(604) 222-5208
Fax:(604) 222-5283 Telex: 0451233

You find the details below in a reference book.

Philadelphia USA. Largest city in Pennsylvania, and 4th largest in the USA, on the Delaware R. at the confluence with the Schuylkill R. Pop. (1980) 1,688,210. A leading seaport, second in importance to New York, with 60 km (37 m.) of waterfront along the two rivers. Many industries. The most famous building is Independence Hall (1732–41), the old State House of Pennsylvania, where the Declaration of Independence was adopted and signed (1776) and the US Constitution was drawn up. Seat of the University of Pennsylvania (1740), the Temple University (1884), and the Drexel Institute of Technology (1891). Founded (1682) by William Penn, who named his city Philadelphia ('City of Brotherly Love') to emphasize the religious and political tolerance he intended to promote. The Quaker influence of the founder is still in evidence, as is also the somewhat conservative and sedate outlook of the inhabitants. A further characteristic distinguishing Philadelphia from most other large American cities is the preponderance of houses as against apartments.

Vancouver Canada. Largest city in British Columbia, the third largest in Canada, and the country's chief Pacific seaport, on Burrard Inlet of Georgia Strait. Pop. (1981) 414,281 (metropolitan area 1,310,600). Has an excellent natural harbour. Commercial, financial, and industrial metropolis of W Canada. International airport. Many fine parks and open spaces, inc. Stanley Park (364 ha). Seat of the University of British Columbia (1908). Before the 2nd World War most of its inhabitants were of British extraction, but since 1945 it has become more cosmopolitan.

Reply to your colleague, indicating which you think would be best for Sonia and explaining why. You may add your own ideas but you should not alter the given facts. Write about 250 words.

SECTION B

*Choose **one** of the following tasks. Your answer should follow exactly the instructions given. You are advised to write approximately 250 words.*

1. A company in your home town is planning to recruit several English-speaking employees and the Personnel Department is preparing an information booklet about your community. You have been asked to contribute a section on an aspect of local life, such as education, medical care or sports facilities. Write a detailed account which will tell a newcomer and his family all they need to know about **one** of these subjects.

2. You recently witnessed an incident in which an animal was treated cruelly. Write an article for your student newspaper, describing what you saw and urging readers to take action against such abuses.

3. You and a friend wish to start a new business. Write a brief account of your plans to put before a group of businessmen who may be interested in helping you to finance your venture. You should describe what your firm will do and explain why you think it will be successful.

4. You receive this letter from some school children in England:

> ... We are a class of 8-10 year olds and we are doing a project about customs and traditions in different countries. Do you have time to help us? Please can you write about one traditional day in your country? Please tell us about the food, clothes and everything.
>
> Thank you very much.
>
> from
>
> Class 4,
> Egmont Middle School.

Write a description to help them with their project.

PAPER 3   ENGLISH IN USE   (1 hour 30 minutes)

Answer all questions.

SECTION A

1   *Read the extract below and circle the letter next to the word which best fits each space. The first answer has been given as an example.*

I don't want to alarm you. There is still ....*enough*.... sand left in the world to satisfy most holidaymakers but in many parts of the world beaches are literally being (1)............................ away and have to be regularly (2)............................ .

First much of the sand for beaches (3)............................ from cliffs which crumble away as they are pounded by the waves. To (4)............................ them, sea walls are often erected. With cliffs no (5)............................ crumbling, the beaches are robbed of the material which would (6)............................ feed them.

Beaches are also (7)............................ with sand and gravel by rivers which bring it down from the mountains and hills. In some places rivers are being dammed and (8)............................ built to retain water. They trap more of the sediment so the rivers (9)............................ less sand and gravel to the sea. This is happening in California, for example, and in Scotland. In Egypt the (10)............................ of the Aswan Dam has (11)............................ the Nile silt, so much less silt is being fed towards coastal (12)............................ . That has meant the delta is now eroding instead of (13)............................ as before.

Thirdly, to improve access to the beach many holiday resorts build a promenade along the sea front. Like some of the fortifications of cliff (14)............................, this usually has a flat vertical surface off which the waves (15)............................ . This helps wash the sand away down the beach and most of it is lost.

	A	much	B	more	Ⓒ	enough	D	some
1.	A	thrown	B	rubbed	C	washed	D	cleaned
2.	A	removed	B	replaced	C	rebuilt	D	redrawn
3.	A	collects	B	forms	C	falls	D	comes
4.	A	protect	B	prepare	C	surround	D	cover
5.	A	sooner	B	longer	C	further	D	later
6.	A	normally	B	often	C	sometimes	D	occasionally
7.	A	presented	B	given	C	filled	D	supplied
8.	A	reservoirs	B	canals	C	wells	D	locks

⟫→

9.	A	fetch	B	take	C	pull	D	push
10.	A	designing	B	engineering	C	building	D	forming
11.	A	kept	B	trapped	C	sealed	D	solidified
12.	A	beaches	B	resorts	C	areas	D	parts
13.	A	growing	B	shrinking	C	swelling	D	reducing
14.	A	tops	B	faces	C	features	D	hangings
15.	A	bounce	B	jump	C	splash	D	ripple

2 *Complete the following extract from an article about hang-gliding by writing the missing words in the spaces provided. Use only **one** word in each space. The first answer has been given as an example.*

Hang-gliding is the modern equivalent of the Icarus legend – but rather more practical. Icarus did his best with wings made of wax and feathers, ...*until*........ the sun melted the wax, and down came Icarus, feathers and (1)............................. A hang-glider is made of materials (2)............................ combine strength with lightness – and don't melt. It is not (3)............................ a pair of wings, (4)............................ has rigging wires, battens, a king-post, a keel pocket, a control frame, and not (5)............................, a parachute.

Judy Leden first (6)............................ hooked, quite literally, on a hang-glider when she was (7)............................ twenty. (8)............................ a teenager she had already found plenty of excitement (9)............................ mountain-climbing and scuba-diving. She entered her first major competition and set a (10)............................ world record (11)............................ an out-and-return of 51 miles, which compares well with the men's record.

So (12)............................ is the attraction of (13)............................ off cliffs all (14)............................ the world, from Hungary to the Himalayas, or (15)............................ hauled into the air – just to glide down again?

SECTION B

3 *In most lines of the following text there is one unnecessary word. It is either grammatically incorrect or it does not fit in with the sense of the text. Read the text carefully and then write the word in the space provided at the end of the line. Some of the lines are correct. If the line is correct, indicate with a tick (√) against the line number. Two of the lines have been done for you.*

Caring for your teeth and gums should include avoiding		.......√.......
such sugary drinks and food, especially between meals.		....*such*....
Regularly remove the plaque and debris from off	1.	....
your teeth with a toothbrush. Use a small-headed brush of medium hardness.	2.	....
This type of brush will easily reach to the	3.	....
awkward areas of the mouth.	4.	....
Brush your teeth after each meal, especially more	5.	....
after breakfast and after the last food or drink of the day.	6.	....
Bleeding gums are such a common occurrence that	7.	....
most of people think it is normal. In fact, bleeding	8.	....
and inflammation of the gums are signs of a	9.	....
common disease – periodontal disease – which may	10.	....
gradually destroys the tissues supporting your teeth.	11.	....
Periodontal disease affects teenagers and adults, and	12.	....
is the commonest cause of tooth loss in amongst adults.	13.	....
It is caused by the continued presence of plaque on the teeth.	14.	....

》》》→

4   Read the following notes from a head teacher to her secretary. Using the information given, complete the letter to parents which the secretary has written for the head. Write the missing words in the spaces provided. The first answer has been given as an example. You should use only **one or two words** in each space.

We must let the parents know what's going on about the building work in the main hall which has been causing such disruption to classes this term. They need to know that it'll make it much warmer there for the children. Also, don't forget to tell them that we've managed to get some new blackout curtains with some of the money from the summer fair.

Did you know that Steve Wood has resigned from the Governing Body? This means we should ask if anyone is willing to replace him - they'd like someone who's got children in the Lower School at the moment as there are more parents from the Upper School on the Committee.

The other thing we must mention is the Bring and Buy Sale. It's next Saturday - the 10th of January, I think, and if they want to give us anything - clothing, toys, books etc. - we'd be very grateful. If they bring stuff for the sale they should leave it in your office. Mind you, if it's things like jam, preserves, cakes and so on, perhaps it would be better left in the school kitchen. Encourage them to help on the day, too! I think that's all for the moment.

Dear Parents,

We have to __warn you__ that there is further building work in the main hall for the children to (1)_____ with. However, there should be an (2)_____ in the heating of this rather cold area. Once the work is complete we shall be able to put up the new black-out curtains which were bought from the (3)_____ of the Summer Fair.

Governing Committee

It has been brought to (4)_____ that, due to the resignation of Mr. Steven Wood, there is a (5)_____ on the school's Governing Committee. We would like to (6)_____ parents who are interested in (7)_____ on this body to make themselves known to the school secretary. With this appointment the Governors wish to rectify (8)_____ between parents (9)_____ the Upper and Lower Schools. It would be (10)_____ for a parent with children in the Lower School to (11)_____ the position.

Bring and Buy Sale

The Sale takes place on Saturday, the 10th January. We would be most grateful if parents (12)_____ such things as clothing, toys and books. Please could you (13)_____ in the secretary's office? (14)_____ should be left in the school kitchens. Anyone who is interested in (15)_____ should let the secretary know. We would be delighted!

Thanking you all in advance,
Yours sincerely,

P. J. Tarrot

P.J. Tarrot
Head Teacher.

SECTION C

5 *Read through the following text and then choose the best phrase or sentence given below, to fill each of the gaps. Write one letter (A–P) in each of the numbered gaps. Some of the suggested answers do not fit at all.*

Every teacher knows that not all students are good examinees. Some are too tense, become over-anxious or too stressed and then perform below expectations (1)............................ .

Teachers try to help by compensating, believing (2)............................ they will cure his fear of exams.

So, last year, (3)............................, I completely rewrote the Business Studies Revision Course at this secondary school. The central idea of the course is to treat the examination as an event, a challenge, a performance, (4)............................, a drama production, or perhaps a major music concert, (5)............................ and very definitely on the public stage. The idea is to show that the exam is not a test, (6)............................ to show how good the candidate is.

The objective is to improve students' final performance (7)............................, control and ability to cope. The theme of 'total preparation for performance' teaches them that (8)............................ are obviously important, they are only two of the five skills required, (9)............................, mental skills and management skills. These additions give a new dimension (10)............................, increasing enjoyment and motivation. They widen a student's focus and help to convince some of the less confident students that there are many ways in which they can actively contribute towards their (11)............................ .

A   much like a sports match
B   self-confidence and self-esteem
C   by increasing self-confidence
D   relying on my expertise alone
E   to a student's revision
F   that if they boost a student's academic knowledge
G   by improving a student's revision
H   but an opportunity
I   those not mattering so much
J   drawing on my teaching experience and sports psychology skills
K   but bigger and more important
L   just when it matters most
M   but a real desire
N   while knowledge and examination techniques
O   despite the need for sustained effort
P   the others being coping strategies

6   *An English-speaking friend has written to ask for some advice in getting a job in catering in London. Using the notes below, construct a reply. You must use all the words in the notes but not necessarily in the same order and you may add words and change the form of the words where necessary. Look carefully at the example which has been done for you.*

a) If work in London, why not look centre – share flat?

b) plenty restaurants around / often advertise staff / noticed experience not necessary always

c) Abigail's, High Street, last week / assistant chef / lunchtimes or evenings / pay low – £3-4 per hour

d) work permit necessary? / check now / arrange interview – next week

e) send personal details / relevant experience / references × 2 / I get started your job application

f) contact soon / next week birthday / party or theatre

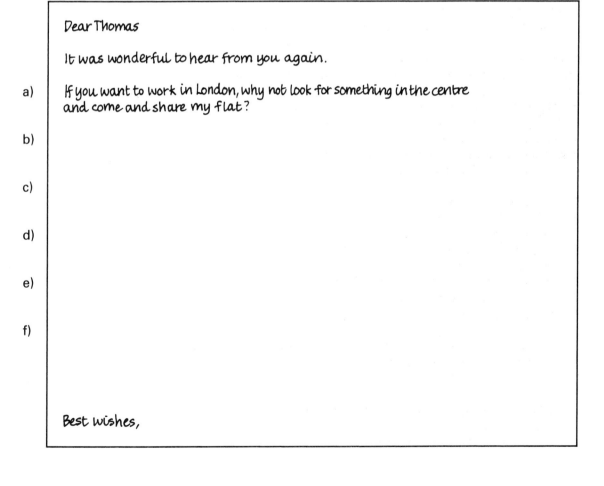

Dear Thomas

It was wonderful to hear from you again.

a)   If you want to work in London, why not look for something in the centre and come and share my flat?

b)

c)

d)

e)

f)

Best wishes,

PAPER 4   LISTENING   (45 minutes)

Answer all questions.

SECTION A

You will hear a recorded message welcoming new staff to the campus and giving them information about the services offered. For questions 1–8 tick those pictures which show you what you should do to receive the appropriate services or to help you keep to the regulations. Listen carefully. You will hear the piece twice.

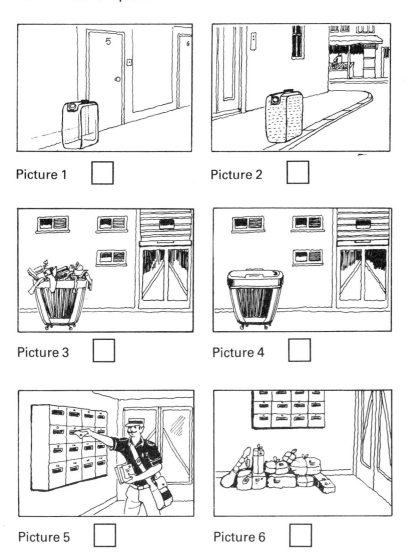

Picture 1 ☐   Picture 2 ☐

Picture 3 ☐   Picture 4 ☐

Picture 5 ☐   Picture 6 ☐

Picture 7 ☐   Picture 8 ☐

SECTION B

You will hear someone giving information about how to travel around Turkey. Look at the sentences 9–17 and complete them by writing one or two words in the spaces. Listen carefully as you will hear this piece once only.

9. It is ☐ 9. ☐ to take a bus than a train.

10. It is possible to travel ☐ 10. ☐ to Istanbul and Izmir.

11. The Blue Train has very comfortable ☐ 11. ☐.

12. It is advisable to book seats during ☐ 12. ☐.

13. In order to find out where the buses are going to you must listen to the ☐ 13. ☐.

14. It is a good idea not to sit on the ☐ 14. ☐ during the summer.

15. All coaches carry ☐ 15. ☐.

16. From time to time you will be offered ☐ 16. ☐ to refresh yourself.

17. Don't expect a good night's sleep as the bus will ☐ 17. ☐.

SECTION C

You will hear an interview with Gerda Geddes, who teaches the Chinese art of movement called 'Tai Chi'. Look at questions 18–22 and tick the best answer, A, B, C or D. You will hear the interview twice.

18. When did Gerda Geddes first become interested in 'Tai Chi'?
    A   when she returned to Norway
    B   in China, forty years ago
    C   during the Cultural Revolution
    D   while visiting Hong Kong

19. What did she feel when she saw the man performing 'Tai Chi'?
    A   She was entranced by the experience.
    B   She thought he was being mysterious.
    C   She thought he looked like a bird.
    D   She felt she wanted to imitate him.

20. Why did she find it difficult at first to find someone to teach her 'Tai Chi'?
    A   because it takes many years to perfect the art
    B   not many people knew about 'Tai Chi'
    C   the Chinese did not want to associate with Westerners at this time
    D   it was usually taught by fathers to their sons

21. What is the main difference she mentions between 'Tai Chi' and more Western forms of dance?
    A   It allows you to concentrate on your breathing technique.
    B   It makes you more supple.
    C   It can prevent damage to the joints.
    D   It uses different sets of muscles.

22. What does she feel is the greatest benefit of learning 'Tai Chi'?
    A   It teaches you to overcome your physical limitations.
    B   It cures physical injuries.
    C   It encourages spiritual growth and awareness.
    D   It postpones the ageing process.

SECTION D

You will hear various people talking. There are five extracts which are not related in any way except that everyone is talking about tourism. You will hear the people twice.

Task 1

For questions 23–27 look at the types of people listed below labelled A–H. As you listen, decide in what order you hear each person speak and complete the boxes 23–27 with the appropriate letter. Three people will not be used.

A   travel agent

B   conservationist

C   holiday-maker

D   hotelier

E   city-dweller

F   tour guide

G   tourist police

H   hitchhiker

23.	
24.	
25.	
26.	
27.	

Task 2

For questions 28–32 look at the topics below labelled A–H. As you listen, put the topics in the order in which you hear them by completing the boxes 28–32 with the appropriate letter. Three topics will not be used.

A   working with tourists

B   summer in the city

C   holidays away from it all

D   restrictions on tourism

E   holiday traffic

F   keeping busy on holiday

G   effect of tourism on the landscape

H   holiday jobs

Topic 1	28.	
Topic 2	29.	
Topic 3	30.	
Topic 4	31.	
Topic 5	32.	

PAPER 5   SPEAKING   (15 minutes)

PHASE A

The examiners will introduce themselves to you and then invite you to talk about yourself.

PHASE B1

Candidate A

The examiner will ask you to describe a picture to your partner, who has a picture which is related to yours in some way. At the end of one minute the examiner will ask your partner to say what the relationship is between the pictures. You will then be able to compare your pictures.

Candidate B

The examiner will ask your partner to describe a picture to you. You must decide how your picture relates to it. After one minute you will be able to compare your pictures.

PHASE B2

Candidate A

The examiner will ask your partner to describe a picture to you. At the end of one minute the examiner will ask you to say which picture your partner has described.

Candidate B

The examiner will ask you to describe a picture to your partner. At the end of one minute your partner will be asked to say which picture you have described.

PHASE C

Candidates A and B

The examiner will ask you and your partner to have a discussion about spending a sum of money. You must reach agreement or agree to differ. At the end of four minutes you will be asked to report your decision to the examiners.

Your education institution or company welfare fund has been given
£25,000 to spend. You are on a committee which must decide how the money
will be spent. Here are some suggestions:
- improve sports facilities, e.g. resurface tennis courts
- more computer software
- better canteen/restaurant facilities
- heating for the swimming pool

You may add more of your own or decide to spend the money in another
way. Decide together how you would spend the money and give reasons for
your choice. Make sure you understand the reasons for your partner's choice.

PHASE D

The examiners will join your discussion and you will be asked more
questions relating to the previous task.

Answer sheet for **Paper 1   Reading**

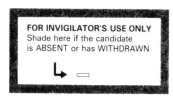
FOR INVIGILATOR'S USE ONLY
Shade here if the candidate
is ABSENT or has WITHDRAWN

Examination/Paper No.

Examination Title

Centre/Candidate No.

Candidate Name

● Sign here if the information above is correct.

● Tell the Invigilator immediately if the
information above is not correct.

MULTIPLE—CHOICE ANSWER SHEET

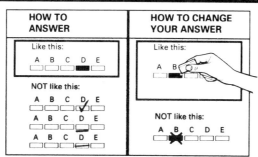

HOW TO ANSWER

Like this:

A B C D E

NOT like this:

A B C D E
A B C D E
A B C D E

HOW TO CHANGE YOUR ANSWER

Like this:

A B

NOT like this:

A B C D E

DO
– use an HB pencil
– rub out any answer
you wish to change

DON'T
– use any other kind of pen
or pencil
– use correcting fluid
– make any marks outside
the boxes

1	A B C D E F G H I J	21	A B C D E F G H I J	41	A B C D E F G H I J
2	A B C D E F G H I J	22	A B C D E F G H I J	42	A B C D E F G H I J
3	A B C D E F G H I J	23	A B C D E F G H I J	43	A B C D E F G H I J
4	A B C D E F G H I J	24	A B C D E F G H I J	44	A B C D E F G H I J
5	A B C D E F G H I J	25	A B C D E F G H I J	45	A B C D E F G H I J
6	A B C D E F G H I J	26	A B C D E F G H I J	46	A B C D E F G H I J
7	A B C D E F G H I J	27	A B C D E F G H I J	47	A B C D E F G H I J
8	A B C D E F G H I J	28	A B C D E F G H I J	48	A B C D E F G H I J
9	A B C D E F G H I J	29	A B C D E F G H I J	49	A B C D E F G H I J
10	A B C D E F G H I J	30	A B C D E F G H I J	50	A B C D E F G H I J
11	A B C D E F G H I J	31	A B C D E F G H I J	51	A B C D E F G H I J
12	A B C D E F G H I J	32	A B C D E F G H I J	52	A B C D E F G H I J
13	A B C D E F G H I J	33	A B C D E F G H I J	53	A B C D E F G H I J
14	A B C D E F G H I J	34	A B C D E F G H I J	54	A B C D E F G H I J
15	A B C D E F G H I J	35	A B C D E F G H I J	55	A B C D E F G H I J
16	A B C D E F G H I J	36	A B C D E F G H I J	56	A B C D E F G H I J
17	A B C D E F G H I J	37	A B C D E F G H I J	57	A B C D E F G H I J
18	A B C D E F G H I J	38	A B C D E F G H I J	58	A B C D E F G H I J
19	A B C D E F G H I J	39	A B C D E F G H I J	59	A B C D E F G H I J
20	A B C D E F G H I J	40	A B C D E F G H I J	60	A B C D E F G H I J

Answer sheet for **Paper 3   English in Use**
[*This is the first sheet only*]

UNIVERSITY OF CAMBRIDGE
LOCAL EXAMINATIONS SYNDICATE
INTERNATIONAL EXAMINATIONS

ENGLISH AS A FOREIGN LANGUAGE

ENTER CANDIDATE
NUMBER HERE

NOW SHOW THE
NUMBER BY
MARKING THE GRID

c 0 ɔ	c 0 ɔ	c 0 ɔ	c 0 ɔ
c 1 ɔ	c 1 ɔ	c 1 ɔ	c 1 ɔ
c 2 ɔ	c 2 ɔ	c 2 ɔ	c 2 ɔ
c 3 ɔ	c 3 ɔ	c 3 ɔ	c 3 ɔ
c 4 ɔ	c 4 ɔ	c 4 ɔ	c 4 ɔ
c 5 ɔ	c 5 ɔ	c 5 ɔ	c 5 ɔ
c 6 ɔ	c 6 ɔ	c 6 ɔ	c 6 ɔ
c 7 ɔ	c 7 ɔ	c 7 ɔ	c 7 ɔ
c 8 ɔ	c 8 ɔ	c 8 ɔ	c 8 ɔ
c 9 ɔ	c 9 ɔ	c 9 ɔ	c 9 ɔ

Examination/Paper No.

Examination Title

Centre No.

ENTER CANDIDATE NAME HERE:

....

● Tell the Invigilator immediately if the
   information above is not correct.

FOR INVIGILATOR'S USE ONLY

· If a TRASNSFERRED CANDIDATE

  Enter original
  Centre No. here   shade here

If an ABSENT or
WITHDRAWN
candidate   shade here

C A E - P A P E R 3 - A N S W E R S H E E T O N E

1		19	
2		20	
3		21	
4		22	
5		23	
6		24	
7		25	
8		26	
9		27	
10		28	
11		29	
12		30	
13		31	
14		32	
15		33	
16		34	
17		35	
18		36	

Continue on **A N S W E R S H E E T T W O**

FOR OFFICE USE ONLY		
81 ⸺ ⸺ ⸺	84 ⸺ ⸺ ⸺	87 ⸺ ⸺ ⸺
82 ⸺ ⸺ ⸺	85 ⸺ ⸺ ⸺	88 ⸺ ⸺ ⸺
83 ⸺ ⸺ ⸺	86 ⸺ ⸺ ⸺	89 ⸺ ⸺ ⸺

Answer sheet for **Paper 4   Listening**

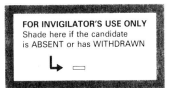

UNIVERSITY OF CAMBRIDGE
LOCAL EXAMINATIONS SYNDICATE
INTERNATIONAL EXAMINATIONS

ENGLISH AS A FOREIGN LANGUAGE

Examination/Paper No.

Examination Title

Centre/Candidate No.

Candidate Name

● Sign here if the information above is correct.

....

● Tell the Invigilator immediately if the
information above is not correct.

LISTENING   COMPREHENSION   ANSWER   SHEET

ENTER TEST
NUMBER HERE →

FOR OFFICE
USE ONLY →

[10][20][30][40][50]

[1][2][3][4][5][6][7][8][9]

1		21		41	
2		22		42	
3		23		43	
4		24		44	
5		25		45	
6		26		46	
7		27		47	
8		28		48	
9		29		49	
10		30		50	
11		31		51	
12		32		52	
13		33		53	
14		34		54	
15		35		55	
16		36		56	
17		37		57	
18		38		58	
19		39		59	
20		40		60	